Brilliant Strategies
and
Fatal Blunders

How Small Businesses
Survive and Thrive
in an
Overcrowded Market

Brilliant Strategies
and
Fatal Blunders

How Small Businesses
Survive and Thrive
in an
Overcrowded Market

Robert E. Krumroy
Author of Identity Branding – Distinct or Extinct

Brilliant Strategies and Fatal Blunders © 2002 by Robert E. Krumroy

I-B Publishing, Greensboro, NC
ISBN: 0-9678661-1-1

Contents

Dedicated to:

Ryan
My son who has taught me the gift of service and
deep friendship.

Taylor
My son who has taught me unconditional love
and to be "me."

Jordyne
My daughter who has taught me compassion, tenderness
and why everyone is worthy of love.

No Greater gifts could a father ever receive.

Acknowledgements

My sincere thanks to the dedicated corps of staff, colleagues, friends and other encouragers who were instrumental in making this book possible. To Michelle Polczynski, our irreplaceable vice president of operations and my number-one cheerleader; to Kelly Grau, the best customer relationship manager we could ever have captured; to George Hiller, a senior executive who as a young man listened, encouraged and believed in me - taking the time to guide my steps while teaching me leadership and compassion; to George Roberts, as faithful a friend as anyone could have; to Betty Work, for her tireless editing contributions; to Marian Stewart, for her endless hours of graphic design work, creative genius and wonderful friendship; and to Bill Heroy, the best photographer in the Southeast.

"Creating YOU as the dominant brand begins by seeing what everybody else is doing and then doing what nobody else has done."

Robert F. Krumroy, "The Branding Coach"

Preface

Mick Zangari
Sr. Vice President, Ameriquest Mortgage
University of Nebraska, Faculty

A sales professional recently shared with me her approach to gaining a competitive market advantage. "It's like an eight-lap race," she said. "You run as fast as you can for the first four laps, and then you aggressively pick up the pace for the last four."

Funny and all too true, her analogy describes the critical speed and all-out effort needed by small businesses and professionals to thrive – or even hang on for dear life – in today's tumultuous and over-saturated markets. Even so, there are ways to create an almost unfair competitive advantage, and this book shows you how to do that.

Robert Krumroy tackles the critical issues involved in building a personal local market brand. He exposes the long-held and antiquated theories on which many businesses and professionals still focus. He gets down to the nitty-gritty of what strategies actually work in today's economy. You'll learn about creating a new form of customer relationship, an emotional bond founded on differentiation. It's a strategy that can clearly separate you from the pack.

Business prosperity is no longer about endurance; neither is it about working harder. It is about dynamic strategy and creativity. Let this book give you the knowledge, energy and secrets to distance yourself from those who would try to take your customers away. The race is getting crowded. Get out front and stay there!

Forward

The Ultimate Winning Edge
And How to Get It

Brian Holloway
President and CEO, H. Center for Competitive Excellence
Former Vice President, NFL Players Association
Five-time All Pro with the New England Patriots and Los Angeles Raiders

Having spent a decade playing in the National Football League, I know a little something about competition. The NFL is, after all, the most competitive culture in the world. Hundreds of thousands of athletes dream of going pro, but by the time the season starts each year, just one hundred and eighty-nine players actually will get the chance to play. Now, that's one tough market. And I'll let you in on a very closely held secret. It's not enough to be fast, big or gladiator tough. In the NFL, these are considered the basics. Everybody has them.

No, succeeding in the NFL takes something more. Something extraordinary that goes beyond the physical. When Marcus Allen, my old Los Angeles Raiders teammate, stepped onto the field, opponents had to prepare for that added dimension that takes the competition to the next level. He brought more to the huddle than any other running back in NFL history.

Which leads us to the million-dollar question. Why do some people consistently excel while others consistently under-produce? Clearly something else must be going on.

This question looms just as large in today's competitive markets for those who sell. How do you outperform the market when all the products and services appear to be identical?

Here's the answer to both. Products are not identical. One McDonald's restaurant will outsell another, despite having the same product, same ideal location, same amount of traffic and same demographics. Teams are not identical either. Only a few are one hundred and ten percent committed to pursuing perfection. The distinct quality, capacity and commitment of Vince Lombardi's Green Bay Packers, Tom Landry's Dallas Cowboys, and Bill Walsh's San Francisco 49ers literally became their identity. They were the best of the best.

> *To outperform the competition, you must find your winning edge.*

This high ideal of "identity" represents the ultimate winning edge. This is what you bring to the game. This is what we, as business owners and sales professionals, must bring to the market. It is the million-dollar secret.

I'm by nature skeptical, not given to endorsing books, projects or services without exercising due diligence. There is nothing worse than another "lotion and potion" book that tells a great story but ends up on the fluff-book shelf, just another tome that fails to deliver on its promise. This book is not one of those.

It didn't take me long to get excited when I learned how Robert had built one of the largest insurance sales agencies in North America. When I looked at how that success was accomplished, it became apparent to me that he possessed a system, a strategy – in short, a winning game plan – that consistently produced extraordinary results. He clearly made a difference in people's lives, because you cannot grow that fast and that big without having the key fabrics of trust, loyalty and passion to hold the organization together during the hard times.

At this particular time in our world's history, we are facing a new, more difficult market economy. To survive, you must be in the business of thinking and strategizing, not just working harder. As challenging as business is today, those with vision can see the new markets of prosperity. New wealth is about to be created, but only for those who take the brakes off their lives, those who decide to participate.

To win in this new environment, you need a very serious marketing strategy that allows you to dominate the market, to be a unique player. That strategy is called Identity Branding, and in this book you will learn how to apply it to your goals and dreams. Believe me, it's the stuff that all dynasties are built upon.

> *Working harder isn't the magic potient for tomorrow's success.*

The worst you can do is stay stuck in the past. I can't tell you how many of my own clients – from Fortune 500 companies all the way down to mom-and-pop stores – are still enamored with strategies that relate to outworn theories of the market and customers. For certain, they're not on the path to the new wealth I'm talking about. As a friend of mine once said: "Being good has nothing to do with making money." There are plenty of good people with good products and good relationships who are consistently under-performing in the market.

I invite you to read this book with great expectations. Take out a pen and write yourself notes in the margins. This is your

Playbook for Success. It may be the most important book you ever read in your business career.

Do not take the easy path. Do more than get in the game to win. Get in the game to unleash your destiny.

Today is day one. It is an awesome day. This treasure of a book is for those people who are committed to getting even better at what they already do very well. Get started and have fun!

Brian Holloway *is an international motivational futurist who earlier enjoyed a stellar career in the National Football League. President and CEO of the H. Center for Competitive Excellence, he counts more than a quarter of the Fortune 500 companies as clients. During his ten years in professional football, Holloway played for the New England Patriots and Los Angeles Raiders and was named All-Pro five times. As vice president of the NFL Players Association, he was one of the principal architects of the football league's growth strategy that posted a landmark eighteen-billion-dollar television contract in 1998.*

"The ability of a business to succeed is far more dependent on the customer's evaluation of the encounter than on the product or service."

Robert F. Krumroy

Answering the Customer's Question: "Why You?"

"I know I can deliver a great product. And if I can do that, plus be ready to sacrifice financially for a year or so, eventually the word will spread. More and more people will notice my quality, my service and my expertise, and business will boom."

Now there's a killer business strategy for you, just brimming with enthusiasm, good intentions, integrity and resolve! In truth, however, it has killed off more potentially great ventures than any other single misconception. So if you've bought into this lethal bit of folklore, be sure to keep your résumé fresh. When your business closes its doors and you're casting around for a job, it will come in handy.

The cold fact is this: In today's market environment, the public is being constantly bombarded with look-alike products and services. Though many are high quality, some even higher than the current competition, the vast majority fails to survive. To customers you are just another fish in an already teeming sea of competition.

This proliferation of "Me-Too" businesses has become the most typical beginning strategy for well-intentioned entrepreneurs starting their own businesses, yet it is the most fatal strategy (if you can call it a strategy) ever pursued. Most "Me-Too" product and service providers rarely produce the sales objectives the entrepreneur originally envisioned. "Me-Too" retail and service businesses rarely yield the profit expectations that accompanied the excitement that birthed their initial endeavor.

Why should they choose you?

So let's step back and consider some realities about the state of the consumer market. There's an incredible amount of competition, and you're all trying to get the attention of customers whose time and patience have worn thin. You need to ask yourself – *why should they choose you?*

Identity Branding is about answering that question. It's about becoming the market leader within your chosen category – the same way that Kleenex, Scotch Tape and Band Aid define and own their categories. This must be your focus, your objective. *Identity Branding* is about making you the competitor that other companies chase, the one that consumers regard as the brand of choice, the company that is regarded as the best, relegating everyone else to no better than second place. Best of all, *Identity Branding* is about positioning you at the top of your game, not only in recognition but also in profitability.

Identity Branding is not an art. It is a science. It is a strategy anyone can learn and employ, not requiring special intuition or innate marketing gifts. It is not a God-given-mystical-gift that a few individuals receive at birth. The one strength you will need is the determination to develop a branding plan and then carry through on it.

Previous experience in business might already have taught you that excellent products or services are no longer the primary attraction for the average customer. Quality remains important to business people with high integrity, but it no longer can be counted on to get you where you want to go. Without a differentiated identity, your business is purely and simply living on borrowed time.

Success is no longer dependent on your ability to find a product hole to fill for your customer. As Lynn Upshaw, author of *Building Brand Identity*, has pointed out, it's about finding "a mind to fill." And great name recognition is no longer enough. You have to give people a reason to buy from you instead of the look-alike competition.

In a society that has produced so many products and services that seem to do the same thing, you either have to be first or you have to be different in order to capture the slightest degree of attention. Sergio Zyman, author of *The End of Marketing as We Know It*, sums it up exactly: "Differentiation is critical; sameness has no value." And as *Marketing Aesthetics* authors Bernd Schmitt and Alex Simonson state: "When products or services are perceived as undifferentiated … experiences become the key selling point."

> *The customer's primary attraction to you is not your product or service.*

Gaining a competitive advantage is never accomplished by chasing the leader; doing the same thing they are doing, only trying to do it better. If you all look relatively the same, where is the incentive for consumers to climb off the wagon they're on in order to ride on your wagon? Differentiation is the foundation of choice, and there are no exceptions. It applies to every business, whether you're a retailer, service provider, consultant, professional or salesperson.

If you don't differentiate, look for a future that's at best mediocre. That is, if you survive. And a quick death might be better than the muddling existence your non-planning, non-differentiated journey will deliver.

Creating your business as the local *brand of choice* always begins by focusing on what makes you distinctive from the competition and then making sure prospective customers get the full impact of a powerful first impression. When business differentiation is soundly established and visibly unique, you will have created dominant attraction and marketplace customers will begin thinking of your competition as shallow. Yes, they will redefine the competition as less desirable when you are successful at accentuating your market differentiation.

> *You will need to accentuate your differentiation to outclass the competition.*

Building a brand preference is never accomplished by creating a "Me-Too" business that tries to do something better than the others, even if you are committed to doing it exceptionally better. The operative words that most failed business owners don't heed are *exceptional differentiation and memorable experience.* Long-term customer relationships are initiated based on emotion, not logic. Features, benefits, advantages and even price (the "intrinsics" of your product) deliver considerably less of an influence on consumer preference than the "extrinsics" – consumer expectation, the experience, your differentiation and the emotional connection created by your business.

You have to be ready to help the customer make that emotional connection. It won't just happen on its own. A well-planned, consistent, repetitive identity-branding strategy aimed at *specific* customers and prospects will give you an excellent chance to create brand preference and a psychologically dominant competitive advantage.

This book's primary purpose is far beyond offering ideas on how to implement new operational or cost-efficiency techniques for your business. Neither is it about traditional branding ideas that focus on name selection, logos, Web sites, brochures or hard-copy advertising. Frankly, mastering these tools will not create the kind of customer pull that will allow you to take local market share.

Don't be another faceless "Me-Too" company.

Likewise, this book does not involve itself with core competencies, total quality management or providing service "beyond expectations." None of these create irresistible appeal in today's market. Traditional ingredients do not provide the formula you need to soar to the top. Until you *Identity Brand* your business to your most desirable customers and prospects, you will be perceived as just another faceless company in an overcrowded sea of competition.

Traditional businesses still want to believe they can promote and sell products based on features, benefits and advantages that are above and beyond what the competition offers. They believe people will eventually recognize theirs as the best product and it will sell like hotcakes. But in a world where advertising noise clutters every minute of every day and claims are made by everyone about everything, selling product attributes and benefits no longer suffices. They no longer draw the consumer's attention into a mode of open-minded inquiry, necessary for making a sale.

In contrast, the new "great companies" focus on building quality perceptions and selling the experience. For these growth-explosive newcomers, the "experience" becomes the key selling point, adding such value to the offering that it creates an almost unfair competitive advantage.

Without an exceptional, surprising and delightful differentiated identity, there is no customer attraction and precious little customer loyalty. Your only recourse would be to compete on price, and that's a losing strategy. If you do not consciously manage your *Identity Brand*, you eventually will look like another "Me-Too" organization. The landscape is littered with businesses that

> *Focus on the experience you deliver.*

chose to ignore this issue. But you don't have to let it be your epitaph.

Identity Branding is not about promoting your product, advertising your product, bragging about service or making claims about expertise. It is a dynamic strategy, not an isolated element that is never revised, reviewed or revisited. It always has a beginning and never an end – at least, not if you intend to prosper now and into the future.

Most academic researchers have failed to address this issue except in esoteric fashion. They have failed to address the strategic principles, much less the management issues that can be identified and implemented. Business schools are still caught up in hard skill curricula targeted to their students: flexible-versus-sequential product development, empathic product-design technique processes, creating value edge in pricing, product lifecycle cost analysis … ad nauseum. All of it is based on 1970 business theory; none of it addresses the attraction process of customers in today's environment.

In contrast, this book is filled with applications and numerous real-life business examples. It is about how to build a quality perception, leave a memorable mark and create a differentiated character in the marketplace.

In *Marketing Aesthetics,* Schmitt and Simonson note that

"consumers are bombarded with hundreds of visual and verbal identity elements every day... they cannot possibly notice and pay attention to all... they selectively choose to focus on some of them and ignore others. Memory errors commonly result...."

The objective of this book is to make sure that "memory errors" do not occur, at least in the matter of where your customer and prospect preferences are concerned. People may never remember all the features and benefits of a product they purchase, but we can make sure they maintain an ongoing familiarity that connects with emotional needs and continues to build their loyalty to your business. This is the business journey you want to take. It's a journey that can yield all the objectives you ever imagined and more.

> *Most of today's academic business theory is not customer-driven.*

Introduction

Summary Reflections

Working harder is no longer sufficient for growing or even surviving your business.

Consumers consider most products and services to be look-a-likes, offering far more sameness in today's market than difference.

The best products don't always survive, and the best service providers often attract little attention.

Claiming to be "best" is a loosing strategy. It causes more skepticism than advantage.

The customer's answer to the question, "Why should I choose you?" is greater than the components of your product or service.

Without a differentiated identity, your business is living on borrowed time. It is just another "faceless" company in an overcrowded sea of competition.

Gaining a competitive advantage requires creating a perception of exceptional differentiation and then accentuating it.

When you are successful at accentuating your market differentiation, the consumer will redefine the competition as less desirable.

Your focus must be on helping the customer make an emotional connection, not a product connection.

"Great companies" place their main focus on selling the experience, not the product or service.

Brilliant Strategies Notebook

My thoughts on how to apply this chapter's lessons to my business...

"Becoming market dominant is
not about thinking better
than the competition.
It is about thinking differently."

Robert F. Krumroy

A New Game
...with New Rules

Remember the days when product performance was considered the be-all and end-all of advertising campaigns? And when the ultimate marketing strategy involved comparing your product or service with that of the competition? It was all based on the belief that customers were fixated on quality above all else. That naturally led people to think that performance was the number-one differentiator in establishing marketplace dominance.

Well, in case you haven't already noticed, dramatic change has gripped retail and service companies in America. Building brand dominance on product performance, when no company today can sustain a competitive advantage for more than six weeks, is an act of futility. If your product or service benefit delivers a wow factor today, the competition will be able to match it in six to twelve weeks – and they will have improved on it.

> *Brand dominance doesn't occur because of product performance.*

As a result, there is no such thing as a product competitive advantage in today's market. Leastways, not one that can be sustained for more than three months – max! And this dizzying state of affairs means that product performance and benefits no longer deliver the consumer pull they once did.

You may have already felt the effects of consumer change and wondered whether it is your imagination or that running a business is just a lot tougher than it used to be. It's definitely not your imagination. The rewards are still there, but the game and the rules are different from those of twenty, ten or even five years ago. It's time to move beyond the "Me-Too" mindset, which has been the death knell of so many businesses, and learn to play by the new rules. The path to high-level success begins with creating a customer belief that you are special, different and unique and then leveraging this focused branding to build a loyal customer base.

Most companies still operate under the assumption that product (or service) is more important than perception, but it needs to be the other way round. Dominating your market doesn't mean you have to prove your product is better than somebody else's. If you think that the best product always wins and that all you have to do is deliver a better one to eventually dominate your market, explain the dominance of Coca-Cola. Its competitor, Pepsi, has clung with unflagging loyalty over the years to blind taste tests that purportedly prove that most consumers prefer their soft drink to Coke. The "Pepsi Challenge" is trotted out time after time, and what does it prove? Not much, apparently. Coke remains the dominant cola in America today – actually in the entire world.

The Campbell Soup Company is another powerful example of how perception rules in the marketplace. For decades, Campbell has been the brand of choice in the canned soup market. But do people really believe it's the best soup on the supermarket shelf? Hertz has the same advantage over its rental car competition. But does being Number One mean that Hertz is measurably better than Avis, Budget or Enterprise? To all of the above, I can only say that I really doubt it.

The truth is that the secret of their success lies elsewhere. These market leaders understand their brand in a radically different way – not as a product or service but as an "emotional connection." In the past, product brands were built on "b" words – bigger, better, best, benchmarking. Now, they're built on "tion" words – emotion, connection, familiarization, differentiation. Today's winning business objective is to capture the spirit: wrapping the product or service around an encounter that creates an emotional connection with the consumer and enriches the texture of their lives.

> *Brand dominance is based on an emotional connection.*

Why the '70s Still Influence Today's Business Theory

From the late 1950s to the 1970s, the world witnessed a proliferation of products more dazzling than any other time in history. The majority of these goods grew out of technical breakthroughs spawned during the heady era of space exploration. We got color TVs and TV dinners; transistors, personal PCs, microwave ovens, McDonald's®, Velcro, plastic, rayon, Gore-Tex, even the Weber grill – to name a few. The resulting business growth and profits from those years made more product development an imperative for virtually every company.

Before 1960, however, American-made products in general had a quality problem. Irritated consumers complained loud and long about the "lemons" they had bought. They wanted more than a salesperson's word that a product did what it was supposed to do. They were outraged by what they considered intentionally false claims. Congress eventually took action, giving consumers a new weapon against manufacturers in the form of extended warranties.

The product warranty wasn't a positive experience, and neither was it a voluntary goodwill gesture extended by the manufacturer, at least not at first. It's no wonder that local merchants who promoted personal guarantees on products they sold flourished during this era. People were more comfortable trusting the store owner than the product. Consumers saw the merchant as their only hope if the product broke or didn't work as promised.

Then, in the 1960s, American manufacturing began tackling the quality problem at its source. Companies adopted quality assurance programs and tied new employee incentive and compensation programs to "zero defect" goals. This quest for quality resulted in world-class goods that local retailers no longer needed to personally stand behind. These were products that could stand on their own. Quality and performance expectations acquired a new legitimacy, a new respect and increased confidence from the consumer.

How the Mega-Retailers Got Their Start

The emergence of quality products during the early 1960s – and the resulting growth in consumer confidence – gave Kmart® an idea that would knock the retail world on its head. Since product quality now stood on its own and local retailer trust was no longer the deciding factor for purchasing, as it had been in years past, why not take advantage? The retailer capitalized on a new strategy of buying in mass quantities and undercutting local stores' prices. A daring and highly effective differentiator was born: low price.

Kmart opened its first store in 1962. Wal-Mart wasn't long in following, opening its first store in 1969. The two chains' strategies were similar, but Wal-Mart added a couple of new elements that made it stand out. They coupled low prices with higher quality merchandise and a nicer environment – and they initiated the shopping experience by posting "greeters" at the door.

By 1970, the price war spawned by these mega-stores was fully underway, and small retailers jumped on the bandwagon. With the likes of Kmart and Wal-Mart focusing their advertising on product and price, merchants felt they had no choice but to follow suit. Nearly every type of business started using loss leaders to lure shoppers into their stores in expectations of selling enough other products to make a profit. It was, of course, a disastrous strategy, one that wiped out innumerable small retailers and service companies.

But what about trust? Didn't trust spawn a lot of business growth in the good old days, not only for a number of large retail companies but also for a lot of small merchants? Didn't we buy products from companies in the belief that we could return an item if it was found to be unsatisfactory? The answer is yes. It wasn't just a small-business strategy. Sears and Nordstrom extracted great customer loyalty with their no-hassle return policies. But as noted earlier, that strategy began losing its punch as quality products emerged in the 1960s.

> *When you make "low price" your attraction, start picking out your casket.*

The Business Theory Oversight

By the mid-1970s, business practice focused on two elements. One was creating customer pull in order to get in front of a potential customer. The second was learning how to sell the product or service by promoting its features and benefits during the encounter. This seemed to work fine for about twenty years, to the mid-1990s. Until then, incomes grew rapidly, even though inflation was right behind, and Baby Boomers were earning college degrees in quantities never before seen.

> *Discard your old ideas. Building consumer preference requires a whole new strategy.*

But in 1973, an event occurred that ushered in a whole new strategy for influencing how consumers purchased products. That year, Ford made its first telemarketing phone call, introducing the public to a future whirlwind of intrusion marketing techniques, along with a barrage of junk mail that has exploded and continues its ugly propagation even today.

By the mid-1990s, this deluge of marketing tactics had turned Americans into a nation of irritated skeptics. Consumer telephone and mail fraud climbed to more than forty-six billion dollars in 1998, and the public responded by embracing brand name products like never before. Small business owners, service vendors and outside sales professionals who relied on "cold calling" were especially affected. Their ability to even get appointments with potential clients they had never met was negatively impacted. When any salesperson called, it had become totally acceptable to just hang up, regardless of whether family or friends were in the room. There was no longer any embarrassment. Just irritation.

You would think that the winds of change would have been recognized by now and that business would have reacted accordingly. But that simply is not the case. During the 1960s and '70s, when most of today's executives were in college, university business curricula emphasized product development and management almost exclusively. After all, that's where the profits were being made. Marketing was highly recognized by the business departments, but only as the science for determining what kind of products consumers should be attracted to if they were developed and then determining how to increase consumer pull to the product or service. It was therefore relegated as a corporate issue, not an issue for the sales department to worry about. After all, new products dazzled the consumer, and national advertising was the primary means for getting noticed.

Until about 1980, we adhered to a belief that if you had a great product, you didn't need to market it. Well, the 1980s are over, though unfortunately it appears that some companies have yet to be informed. Nearly every company during those years thought that advertising was the major component for creating consumer pull. That's the main reason why creating initial attraction to a product was relegated as being a corporate issue, not a local selling issue. We believed that the corporate and national home offices could advertise on TV and in magazines and the public would respond.

> *Don't get duped! Media advertising generates less consumer-pull.*

The result was that companies sharply separated the marketing department (which would have been more appropriately named the advertising and promotion department) from the sales and distribution department. When sales dipped, business executives were taught to first check all the elements of their product competitiveness: features, benefits, advantages and price. The only other corporate possibility was advertising. Maybe advertising wasn't creating enough consumer pull, like it was supposed to. If all of that was satisfactory, the problem was conclusive: It had to be a distribution problem. The solution was to improve sales training or sales management. Boy, were they wrong.

What Happens when Customers Give Up

> Claiming to be "Best" creates customer skepticism.

To further exacerbate this issue, the flood of "Me-Too" products created a perception of parity. Swamped and skeptical, consumers attached themselves to leading brands at an unprecedented rate. Of all the choices on America's shelves, name brands accounted for ninety percent of all product purchases by the end of the 1990s.

According to Jack Trout, author of *Differentiate or Die*, the typical grocery store today stocks more than forty thousand products. Despite all that variety, a meager one hundred and fifty of these products ring up more than eighty-five percent of the sales. This has happened because people are no longer concerned about making the "best" choice. Best has become a relative term for today's consumer; claims of "best" are always viewed with skepticism. Consumers are more concerned about not wanting to make a "bad" choice.

The consumer is exhausted. Consider what Jack Trout found in comparing today's marketplace with that of 1970. Today, we can choose from:
  • One hundred and forty-one brands of pain reliever, compared with seventeen

- Twenty-nine brands of toaster pastry, compared with three
- Sixty-four types of dental floss, compared with twelve
- An average of one hundred and eighty-five TV channels if you have cable, compared with five

So many choices and a growing unwillingness to evaluate new ones and to be open-minded. People have mentally surrendered. Enough is enough!

So what has been the final result? People are less patient, more irritated and more skeptical due to the onslaught of more products, more advertising and more intrusion marketing methods than ever before. The outcome is that consumers, whether consciously or unconsciously, have a new criterion when making a purchase. When their interest is aroused by a potential need or desire for a product, they are more attentive to the experience they are purchasing than the product attached to it. After all, most products are pretty much the same. If they have lasted for any period of time, they must have a degree of quality and sameness – at least that's the perception of today's consumer. Once a need is concluded, just about any quality product will do. It's the experience that a customer encounters that becomes the primary determinant for deciding whom they will purchase from.

Therefore, if you continue to think that the best product or service will eventually rise to the top, you will lose. If you think your company's national brand name recognition will cause a prospect to buy, you will continue to be disappointed. And increasing product selection or adding services may be the worst strategy you can implement.

> *Best products and services don't win the business.*

The intensification of choice in today's market has not

increased people's ability to make a buying decision. The increase in choice has actually decreased their willingness to evaluate new products and to be open-minded. The saying that goes "My mind is made up; don't confuse me with the facts" is truer today than it ever has been.

In an over-communicated society, perceptions are formulated faster than ever before. Perceptions – conclusions we draw based on partial pieces of information – simply substitute for not having enough time to evaluate all of the information in the market. When information overload kicks in – when we hit our saturation point – we jump to hard-and-fast conclusive perceptions in order to simplify our lives. A world of choice may be an American value that we expect, but when there are too many choices and the amount of information is overwhelming, we formulate perceptions more quickly and on less information. When there is too much to read and too much to follow up on or keep up with, choice becomes paralyzing. We know that when choices become too many, our coherent ability to evaluate them eludes us. Choice becomes a state of siege, not of freedom.

> You can't over-communicate your difference.

Whether consciously or unconsciously, consumers have come up with a formula that works for them. And it's not about sorting through the fine points of merchandise. Competing products are seen as pretty much the same. What does matter to them is the experience.

Marketing is no longer "just about knowing your customer," says Jack Trout in *Differentiate or Die*. "It is about your customer knowing about you." It doesn't happen through increasing your business's name recognition. It does happen through building intrigue and making your business look distinctively different from the rest of the competition. Differentiating the consumer's encounter is what creates brand attraction and adds depth to a company's name or a product's name. The degree of your differentiation will eventually be reflected in the degree of your customer appeal.

Why Service and Expertise Claims Don't Work

In order to thrive in the future, it is imperative that you create a differentiation relative to the competition and then announce, proclaim, brag about and accentuate it. You can't over-communicate your difference.

But to complicate things more, differentiation that attracts customers in today's market is usually much more than product or even service differentiation. Claiming service superiority as your difference is no more desirable to listen to than salespeople who insist on dragging a customer through a product comparison pitch. And, candidly, engaging in a superior product or service dialog is the fastest way to aggravate and alienate a future customer. It simply reinforces that you are playing the same game as your competitors, and frankly customers don't welcome or even believe claims of this type.

> *Service is important, but it is not an initial business attraction.*

You might regard your service as the best in the world. To customers, though, good service is anything but a differentiator. It's expected. And if it isn't delivered, the customer will leave. If people are attracted to your business because of service, it's because someone else repelled them.

Additionally, trying to use expertise as a differentiator suffers from the same problems. Claiming to be "best" at anything today is viewed with skepticism. It's not the topic of a welcomed conversation. It is not that good product and service aren't important, but prospective customers have no way to judge the facts.

Having eliminated best product, best service or best expertise as winning strategies, you must be wondering what does work. The answer is this. Having the best quality perception is what wins! It's worth repeating what Lynn Upshaw in *Building Brand Identity* said about this because it's so elementary and so true. "You no longer have a product hole to fill. You have a mind to fill."

Chapter One

Summary Reflections

No company can build a lasting attraction based on a product feature advantage.

In today's world of information technology, the competition will match your product feature advantage and improve on it within six weeks of introduction.

Your businesses' experience perception is more important than your product or service.

One of the most vicious business killing myths in America is that given enough time, the best product or service in a business category will eventually rise to the top and the consumer will reward you with their business.

Claiming to be "best" is viewed with skepticism. Consumers are more concerned about not wanting to make a "bad choice" than making the "best" choice.

Today's winning business objective is to create an emotional connection with the consumer.

Competing on price (even if only to attract initial attention) is eventually a fatal strategy for small business owners.

Increasing product selection in your business or adding services may be the worst strategy you can implement. You can't accentuate a distinction with an "everything" business or store. Once you're an "everything," price is your only differentiator. And attempting to be the low price leader is not a long-term survivable strategy for the small business owner or service provider.

Differentiating the consumer's encounter, which gives the perception of gaining a superior advantage if I do business with you, is what creates dominance over the competition in today's marketplace.

Brilliant Strategies Notebook

My thoughts on how to apply this chapter's lessons to my business...

"You can't follow the competition
and expect to gain a
competitive advantage."

Robert F. Krumroy

Chapter Two

The Four Business Platforms

Until around 1940, life in the United States was fairly basic. Most people worked on farms, in day-to-day product manufacturing or in service jobs. Few people traveled. Television was a novelty. There wasn't much "extra" money, and product purchases followed natural need – supply and demand, as economists would say.

But the age of consumerism wasn't far off. Americans began enjoying greater prosperity after World War II. At the same time intellectual resources were being directed to research and development, influenced by science and technology developed during the war. We began to see products and services that far

Today's survival principles have been drastically redefined.

surpassed the definition of basic. Advertising would become more than an occasional street billboard sign or a painted sign on the side of a barn. Our contemporary society was about to be born.

In the decades since then, the principles for surviving in business have undergone an enormous restructuring. And you would have expected businesses to change with them. But all too often, even despite deteriorating economical fundamentals, many have not. Maybe fighting for survival is all they can manage, with no time to consider strategy, innovations or creating a contemporary foundation necessary for success. The consequences are reflected in the many business contractions, mergers and acquisitions, the continuing erosion of company financials, and sometimes a company's total demise.

To address this issue in a meaningful way, we need to understand the four basic business foundations and determine where in the mix they fit. All businesses, knowingly or unknowingly, fit into one of these four modes. The problem is that not all of them are survivable in today's market, regardless of commitment or extraordinary effort. Old strategies may have worked for years, producing satisfactory results. It's natural to cling to the belief that a little tweak here or there will put profits and growth back on track. But as you will see, the change we're talking about is way too big for a little tweak.

The "Me-Too" Focus

This is the oldest principle for a business foundation, established on the premise that the market is big enough for "Me-Too." It was a survivable strategy from the late 1940s to the 1960s. During those years, the post-war Baby Boom created a growing demand for all kinds of products, and this in turn made room for lots of new competitors. There was plenty of business to go around. There were plenty of eager customers.

> A "Me-Too" business strategy will prove fatal.

Then came inflation. At least initially, this new phenomenon actually provided more purchasing power than damage for the average consumer. As wages rose, Americans were quick to spend the extra cash in their pockets. We became two-car families. More "Me-Too" businesses came into existence to meet demand and provide convenience. There was an ancillary impact on the professional services sector – dentists, doctors, lawyers and insurance providers. We could afford these luxuries, and demand for them flourished.

Inflation also quickly redefined insurance needs, and the average family – owning less than fourteen thousand dollars worth of life insurance in 1973 – was not a difficult target. Insurance sales forces grew dramatically, as did agent solicitations. The opportunities were huge, even as a "Me-Too" company. Those were the days when you could just about sit back and let the customers find you.

The "Me-Too-But-Better" Focus

This was the most common business foundation in the 1980s. The premise for it went something like this: "We fully acknowledge that 'Me-Too' is not good enough, but if we combine it with 'better' product features and benefits and 'better' quality service, we will have a winner."

> *A "Me-Too-but-Better" strategy never creates a competitive advantage.*

Many companies continue to operate on this foundation, believing that customers are paying attention to their claims of "better," especially if they can prove it. If they are still surviving with this business belief, it's because old customers, like old habits, are hard to kill. But trust me, most businesses based on old customers are serious candidates for the terminal ward. A closer look at their operating pictures usually shows a struggle, especially among service providers.

The sales people have to work harder just to stay even in getting new customers or getting in to see prospects, and when the numbers drop, their selling skills are called into question. They know better – though not many of them would tell the boss that. They know the owners or sales management tend to discount the seriousness of it being harder to see prospects as the "real" cause of declining sales (after all, they have been successfully training the sales force the same way for as long as they can remember), or they condescendingly scoff at its effect when presented, as though it weren't a "real" issue.

> *There are no customers looking for a "Me-Too" company.*

Regardless of your evaluation to this input, the facts are that people have become more hesitant today about trying something new, even if you can prove it is better than what they have been accustomed to. Is it skepticism? Too many broken promises? Too many advertising claims? Too much to do in life and not enough time to evaluate new stuff? (After all, the old stuff worked just fine.) It is all of that and more. There is too much product noise in today's market. There are no longer enough customers to go around to support another "Me-Too-But-Better" company. The competition is fighting to take your customers away, not to find new ones. It is time to implement a new business foundation. The "Me-Too-But-Better" strategy is a losing proposition.

The "Excellence" Focus

For some companies, the 1990s brought an awareness that not only were consumers different now but also that the work force had changed. Books such as Scott Peck's, *A Road Less Traveled,* Steven Covey's, *Seven Habits of Highly Successful*

People, and Tom Peter's, *In Search of Excellence,* explored the issues of civility, partnership, empowerment, personal meaning and teamwork. These issues would reshape how consumers, employees and management interacted.

A societal change as well as a consumer change was dictating the need for a new business platform. Many companies were becoming aware that their success would require more than the traditional employee/employer relationship. They responded to this challenge with mission and vision formulation teams, dynamic empowerment workshops and peak performance initiatives. They deepened strategic alliances, created strategic think tanks, held leadership conferences and survival rope course weekends, and sent teams on Outward Bound-type experiences.

The endeavors were valuable, even long overdue, in teaching people to work better together. Even so, none of them addressed the fundamental issue of attracting customers in an over-communicated market. None of them taught the business how to build a prospect highway to a prospect community that has a preference for you. That's right. Not for your product. *For you.*

> *"Operational excellence" is a worthy goal... but not the magic formula for creating a visible point of attraction.*

The experiences talked about above may have produced very efficient work teams and wonderfully motivated people, but they didn't make up for the fact that business fundamentals have changed for good. Employees who interface with customers know they are much harder to reach and to sell. For the most part, the desired goals of higher productivity, greater sales, lowered operating costs and higher profit margins continue to elude businesses. Something is still missing. *Customer attraction!*

The Differentiation Focus

In 1960, there was no competition. Good was good enough. "Me-Too" was adequate, and the strategy worked. In 1980, "Me-Too-But-Better" actually created a competitive advantage that replaced traditional "Me-Too" companies. In the late 1980s and early 1990s, "Excellence" reliably brought home the gold. But over the last few years, all three of these business foundations have come into question. They simply don't work in today's marketplace. "Me-Too" is a death wish. "Better" has been dismissed as exaggeration. "Excellence" may be a survival tactic, but still is not enough to create customer dominance.

> Create a sense of intimacy with the customer.

The new foundation of choice is "Differentiation." It's not about product or service, but about creating a perception of quality in the mind of the consumer. More often than not, it's your ability to create a sense of intimacy with the customer. But it's not just about relationships. In *Differentiate or Die*, Jack Trout describes "exceptional differentiation" as "an attribute that is characteristically unique, distinct and noticeably attributable to you." And he writes that "the more crowded the market, the more distinct your difference must be."

> What makes you distinct, unique and memorable?

Identity Branding is not what you do with your product. It is what you do that makes you distinct, unique and memorable. Your *Identity Brand* takes place in your consumer's mind, not in their knowledge of your product or their concern about your price. I can't emphasize enough the danger of competing on price alone. Price only attracts customers when they "have no other ideas about why [they] should buy your service or product," says Sergio Zyman in *The End of Marketing as We Know It*. Believe it. If price is your strategy, you're not marketing, and it's only a matter of time before the competition puts the squeeze on with lower prices. If you can cut price, so can someone else and eventually that someone else will have the ability to outlast your pain. If you focus on a customer attraction strategy that targets product or price without creating a *differentiated* quality perception, you are going to lose.

Great marketing creates customer preference and builds deep customer loyalty. Getting those results will require you to implement five strategy steps.

- Decide on the image you want to create in your marketplace
- Identify your target audience and find a way to obtain a large number of these prospective customers' names
- Accentuate a differentiation as compared to the competition, giving your audience a reason to look your way
- Astonish your audience at least four times a year
- Create a frequent-connection strategy with your audience

The consumer has to have a good reason to choose you over the competition. How would you answer this question: *"What is the premium the customer gets by doing business with you?"* The new consumer is demanding far more than the old business foundations were capable of providing. What is your distinction and is it visibly identifiable? If you're going to survive, you must respond with a focus on differentiation.

What is the premium the customer gets by doing business with you?

The Foundation of Choice

So what do you offer that creates a perception of being different? The quest for success is about creating a genuine attraction that answers the customer's question, "Why you?" It is about making emotional connections and intensifying relationships on a continuous basis. It's about creating a tremendous emotional competitive advantage and becoming the "Brand of Choice" within your local market. It is not a dream. It is a goal that can be accomplished, but it takes more than just hard work and perseverance.

> *Differentiation is the basis of great marketing.*

Differentiation is the basis of great marketing. In today's world, you simply have to give the customer a reason to choose you. Even though many products or services may look similar, if not close to identical, differentiation is the foundation of choice. It is the deciding factor in making a purchase decision. Usually, that differentiation is not your product. Product no longer wins the sale. It is you, not your product or your service that wins the heart and the customer's attraction. Your uniqueness compared to that of the competition is the biggest deciding factor.

Some of you believe that by just getting better and better, eventually the world will notice and reward you with first-place honors, which include getting "the business." You are mistaken, and this false belief may cost you dearly. We once believed that when a business or professional identity had some degree of longevity attached to it, business would be fairly secure and flowing. That is simply folklore in today's environment. One's attraction identity has little to do with longevity or even talent. It has everything to do with visibility and maintaining a perception of differentiation.

If your image and service packaging looks relatively the same as others, without a visible differentiation, prospects will draw the same conclusion. The conversation in

> *Market attraction has little to do with longevity.*

their minds will go something like this, *"Just another one of those businesses. If you've seen one, you've seen them all. No need to visit or to even engage in a conversation. Been there, done that. I have more important things to do with my time. Besides, I don't have any compelling reason to change who I have done business with in the past. Yeah, this new business could be a little cheaper, but deciding to give my business to my current person was a decision that required some risk on my part. I really didn't know anything about [carpet cleaning, investing, painting, clothing boutiques, web providers, printing, landscaping], and my current provider has done OK, I guess. At least they haven't destroyed anything. And price? I really don't care if they're a little cheaper. At least I feel somewhat safe with whom I'm doing business with now.*

Why complicate my life with having to go through another decision and another salesperson's pitch. It's not like my current provider is the doctor who operated on the wrong organ. I think my current provider is probably as efficient as this new alternative ... so I'll stay with what I know. Plus, I really don't like meeting with people I have never met before or even going into all the new stores. Especially when I have no compelling reason that I know of. At least, I haven't heard anything remarkably different about this other business that I can recall. They just all look the same. And their claims of being better ... I hate those pitches! Give me a break!"

Chapter Two

Summary Reflections

The foundational principles for surviving in business are undergoing an enormous change.

Historically, there are four basic business foundations – one of which every business operates even today, whether knowingly or unknowingly.

1. **"Me-Too"**
   A 1940s to 1960s strategy when plenty of customers, post war wealth and low competition created plenty of room for new providers. It made going into business to grab a portion of "market share" a legitimate business strategy.

2. **"Me-Too-But-Better"**
   An antiquated early 1980s strategy based on a belief that customers wanted facts and comparisons that proved your product or your service superiority over the competition. If your product could be proven to out-match the competition, you would then capture the customer's attention and business.

3. **"Excellence"**
   The 1990s focus on zero product defect, great service and leadership versus functional management. A great movement in the direction of becoming financially more profitable and market driven, but something was still missing. Today, it is still a primary tactic pursued by many companies, but it doesn't build dominance in the

consumer market and neither does it attract new customers.

4. **"Differentiation"**

The new focus is on how to create a sense of emotional intimacy and likability with the consumer. It is not about product or price; it's about what makes you distinct, unique, likable and memorable in the customer's mind. It answers the question, "What's the premium the customer gets by doing business with you?"

Brilliant Strategies Notebook

My thoughts on how to apply this chapter's lessons to my business...

_____

_____

_____

_____

_____

_____

_____

_____

_____

_____

_____

_____

_____

_____

_____

_____

_____

_____

_____

_____

_____

_____

_____

_____

"Customer preference is very rarely founded on the factual comparison of products or services. It is usually the result of what the customer believes the "premium" is that they attain by doing business with you."

Robert F. Krumroy

Chapter Three

Becoming a Market Leader While Avoiding the Giant Mistakes

To be a market leader, according to Michael Treacy and Fred Wiersema in their book *The Discipline of Market Leaders,* you have to excel in at least one of three categories: product leadership, operational excellence or customer intimacy.

But beware! Though the reasoning is sound as far as the rise of the giant retail and service chains is concerned, these business attraction models are strikingly dissimilar and can be dangerously misapplied by the local small business owner. Only one of the three models (and even it requires modification) is critical to your plan for becoming a local market brand. Here's an overview of the three and some thoughts on choosing the focus you will need to master.

Product feature and benefit comparisons are practically impossible for the average person to analyze.

Product Leadership

In service and non-consumable retail businesses, where products are infrequently purchased and used, Product Leadership is the most difficult consumer attraction mode to pursue, conquer and then eventually defend. Most products, tangible as well as services, have so many similar alternatives today that consumers shrink from the demands of judging among choices. Even different features and benefits – which the salesperson is so enthusiastic to point out – are practically impossible for the average person to analyze.

> *The general population believes that all products and services are more similar than dissimilar– regardless of your insistence otherwise!*

To further complicate this issue, we're now predisposed to believe that products and services are more similar than dissimilar. Even when there are advantageous differences that might be technically provable, they are more irritating than interesting for most people to hear expressed. Product parity has arrived in the mind of the consumer, and this is where reality exists, not on the retail shelf.

Consumers today are more concerned with not making a bad decision than determining whether or not they have made the "best" decision. We do it all the time. Given the choice of pulling a Coca-Cola out of a soda machine and a no-name alternative – even one that claims to be the number-one winner in a million taste tests – would you take the chance that it's true? You're taking the Coke, regardless of the claim of proof.

> *Consumers are more concerned with not making a bad decision than the "best" decision.*

The bottom line is that people just don't want to be disappointed. Not making a bad choice is far more important for most consumers than evaluating whether they have made the best choice. The result is that product leadership is the most difficult category to attain, particularly so if you weren't first in the market. Creating believability in a newer "best product" – even by communicating proof-positive facts – is virtually impossible. Consumers are not listening. Neither do they care.

Operational Excellence

From the consumers' perspective, Operational Excellence is not an initial attraction that is given much conscious thought – it is assumed to be present. Consumers expect everything to be done well, and they can be infinitely unforgiving when they discover that service is poor, even when explained away as "due to circumstances." There just is no excuse that will suffice when service is disappointing.

When customers are attracted to your company because of operational excellence, it is usually because they had a bad encounter with the people they previously did business with. You may have been fortunate to be in their path as they were fleeing and searching for a new provider, but their attraction to you is far more connected to the flight path than the new destination. This is not meant to minimize your need to provide great operational excellence – if you don't, you will drive your own customers away. But it is hardly a strategy you can use to continually attract new business. In a nutshell, making operational excellence your identifying characteristic for attracting new business is a losing proposition.

> *Service is not an initial customer attractor, it is a potent customer repellent.*

"Another e-tailer could be headed into cyberspace history," said a commentary about Etoys that aired on CNBC's "Squawk Box" in December 2000. David Faber, host of the cable program, shared a personal experience with viewers. "I bought two toys from EToys in 1999 and they got it wrong twice. You don't go back to a place that gets it wrong twice. You go somewhere else..." Putting two and two together adds up to a horrible price to pay for poor service. Need I say more? Service is not an initial customer attractor, but it is a potent customer repellent in an overcrowded marketplace.

To excel in service, don't overlook the importance of promoting your brand internally. Internal brand promotion encourages employees to brainstorm, define and create their own operational *distinction deliverable* where they can feel, see and measure their contribution. If included in creation of the company's annual strategy plan, they can add tremendously to the image of the brand. If excluded, they can just as easily hamper your efforts of becoming the brand of choice.

Customer Intimacy

> *Becoming a local market brand requires creating customer-intimacy.*

Customer Intimacy, the cornerstone of becoming a local market brand, is the most important of the traditional three attraction models for drawing and keeping customers. Brands have no justification for being dominant based on quality. Far more than the sum total of their parts, they create a mystical image that is based on perception. Low price is not a determinant. Actually the opposite is true. The lower the price, the lower the *brand value* and customer loyalty.

Creating the most effective customer intimacy, as a small business, starts with delivering a unique experience to targeted prospects. It is not initiated through print advertising campaigns. Nor is it the result of greater name recognition, larger product choices or enhanced service. It is instead built on whatever allows you to stand out from the crowd, something that is visibly unique and differentiated relative to the competition, something that creates market intrigue. This is then coupled with a strategy that personally, repetitively and consistently connects and influences the customer.

Intimacy is created by distinction, likability and consistent familiarity. There is no substitute. Brands are never characterized by just being better than the competition. Brands become intimate to their users, and users to their brands. They create an emotional bond.

> *Intimacy is created by distinction, likability and consistent familiarity— all three.*

Maintaining a market advantage as a brand requires a commitment to promoting one's distinction. It's a serious job, but it can also be fun and rewarding. It can create an *esprit de corps* within your company that is captivating and personally satisfying for every employee, from the receptionist to the business owner.

But as we'll discuss in the next chapter, creating customer intimacy is still not enough. There is another step if you plan to create a dominant competitive position in today's market.

Chapter Three

Summary Reflections

There are three typical consumer attraction models. Most business owners chose one as their primary focus in attempting to get noticed in their local community.

1 **Product Leadership**
   This is the most difficult strategy to pursue. The average person doesn't have the expertise to judge what is best. Even if your features and benefits are superior, most people believe that product parity has leveled the playing field between companies and products. Product comparisons are irritating to most consumers and cause more skepticism than attraction.

2 **Operational Excellence**
   Great service is expected. It is extremely important. It is like defense on a sport's team. Defense keeps the other teams from scoring against you, from taking your business. Poor service is a potent customer repellent. But, it is not an initial customer attractor. Don't base your initial customer attraction strategy on priding yourself on giving great service. Great service keeps customers. It does not initially attract new business.

3 **Customer Intimacy**
   This is the cornerstone for becoming a local dominant brand. Providing distinction (market separation), likability and consistent familiarity creates intimacy and customer loyalty. It is built on providing a customer

experience - market intrigue - that makes you stand out from the crowd.

Brilliant Strategies Notebook

My thoughts on how to apply this chapter's lessons to my business...

_____

_____

_____

_____

_____

_____

_____

_____

_____

_____

_____

_____

_____

_____

_____

_____

_____

_____

_____

_____

_____

_____

"Becoming market dominant is not about delivering a one-time unique promotional experience.

Market dominance evolves through your strategy of being consistently and uniquely visible to your customers and becoming more likable than the competition."

Robert F. Krumroy

Chapter Four

Distinction Intimacy: The New Face of Success

The traditional business focus – whether on product, operational excellence or even customer intimacy – no longer guarantees success. These belong to a bygone economic era. For the small business owner seeking to become a local market brand, what's needed is a new focus called *Distinction Intimacy*.

Distinction Intimacy is composed of four elements:
1. Promoting a **distinction deliverable** (a visible differentiation that is uniquely yours as compared to the competition)
2. Creating a **unique likability**
3. Operating to **delight the customer**
4. **Consistently communicating** with a specific audience

Branding begins by first deciding what your local differentiation is going to be and then making sure it delivers a "likability" that's different from the competition. It requires that daily business decisions be based not on rigid operating procedures but on delighting customers. And, finally, your distinct personality must be continually

> *You must deliver "likability" that's different from the competition.*

promoted to a defined prospect audience.

There is no substitute for these four elements when creating a *distinction intimacy*. Let's take a closer look.

1. *Distinction Deliverable*

> *Your product is not singularly defined. The customer views it as part of a package of value.*

Consumers no longer view a professional buying relationship as synonymous with purchasing a commodity. They are purchasing an experience, a package of perceived value. Typically, they can't tell you exactly why they chose one product or service over another; they just know that the "whole" is greater than the sum of whatever it was they bought. The power of a brand lies in the mind of the consumer, not in the product portfolio or name recognition. What do you offer that rises above your stock? The greater the differentiation, the greater the appeal.

Building a brand personality requires creating "intrigue" within your market segment. A unique experience is the initial foundation of building brand preference. Doing what the competition is doing, only better, does not create memorable experiences. The successful strategy demands that if the competition is doing "Y," you do "X." If they are going right, you go left. It requires doing different things and doing them differently. It requires innovation, not imitation. It requires leadership that encourages and willingly listens to the "wild ideas of the employees," with a passion to continually find new ways to accentuate their differentiation and uniqueness.

A strong brand mixes and matches different marketing activities and opportunities. It is not dependent on just one thing. Different experiences reinforce consumer awareness and enhance the depth of the brand.

2. *Likability*

We trust people we like. "Likability" is the most important initial element for developing trust in a relationship, and it builds the strongest and most durable perceptions among customers. A consistently friendly demeanor, even during times of crisis or disappointments, is imperative to maintaining customer attraction. Lynn Upshaw notes in *Building Brand Identity*: "A brand's positioning establishes its credibility, but its likability is a direct function of its personality." His counsel: Give customers "something to like" that has substance. Only after determining that they like you will they evaluate whether they trust you.

3. *Delighting the Customer*

One difference between corporate conglomerates and the successful small business is the underlying reason why they pursue a reputation for customer service. Most large companies define error-free service as great service, and they put a lot of faith and resources into accountability tools that let them chart employee performance, measure progress and tie it all to corporate expectations. The tools gather a mass of data – data that many department executives have learned to use for defensive purposes during the infamous annual performance and profitability reviews. In contrast, the small

> *The small business owner figures out a way to say "yes" to any reasonable request.*

business owner pursues great service in order to delight the customer, not for the purpose of measuring corporate improvements. The focus is on figuring out a way to say "yes" to any reasonable request; to deliver more than is expected; to turn the surprised and satisfied customer into an apostle. When employees buy into "the cause" of surprising and delighting their customers, the seeds are planted for becoming a local market brand. That is what causes a small business to grow and thrive, even against the odds that the big conglomerates cast against their continued success.

4. Consistent Communication

Most business owners know that it's sixteen times more expensive to attract new customers than to do repeat business with existing ones. So it's curious that so few go to the trouble of creating a strategy that would allow them to stay connected to their customer base. In a recent survey, more than seventy percent of customers who stopped doing business with a particular merchant or service provider did so because they felt the business had become indifferent to them. In other words, they felt no one cared whether they returned. They regarded their past relationship as superficial – certainly no reason to be committed to you. When the customer doesn't hear from you *frequently*, or if the only time they hear from you is because you're attempting to initiate another business transaction, there is no legitimate relationship, no established depth of loyalty. And, eventually, there is no customer.

> *When the customer doesn't hear from you frequently, their commitment to return fades quickly.*

As in romance, successful small businesses know the

importance of the courting process (staying in touch). Yet very few owners of small or large businesses do it well, if at all. Those who do, however, convey a sense of warmth and caring. They know how to use the consistency of communication tools to great effect. They stay in touch with thank-you notes, phone calls (sometimes just to say hello), newsletters, e-mail messages, postcards, birthday remembrances, annual questionnaires and advance notices for special sales. They build large, name-specific databases of past and potential customers and use them to activate marketing plans that create emotional bonds with these people.

An effective marketing strategy will require accumulating specific customer and hope-to-be customer names in a database.

The great marketers know that their target market is not an impressionistic glance at the demographics within the local area. Rather, their target market is continually individualized. It is built with a focus on accumulating specific names within their market. They realize they can't stay in touch if they can't focus on specific individuals. They cannot provide unique, distinctive and differentiated connections if they don't build a specific name database of potential customers whom they can influence with consistent communication.

Summary Reflections

The new focus for building your business as a dominant brand is creating a Distinction Intimacy that is recognized by the customer.

The four components that make up a Distinction Intimacy are as follows:

- Strategizing Your Distinction Deliverable
- Delivering Unique Likability
- Delighting and Surprising the Customer
- Consistent and Frequent Communication

Eliminate rigid operating procedures that determine how you handle customers. Operating procedures are not hard and fast. They are like anchors that at times need to be picked up and moved depending on the situation.

View what you sell not as your product with its mundane features and benefits but rather as a package of value – an experience - far exceeding the attributes of your product or service.

High-level success requires creating customer intrigue that is "likable."

Great service is about delighting the customer. It is not always about enforcing the company rules or pleasing the financial officer. Allow employees to have "situational authority" when they deem it is necessary. If you hesitate about your employee's judgment, find a new employee.

When the customer doesn't consistently hear from you, (YOU being proactive is the point) or if they only hear from you when you're attempting to initiate another business transaction, their conclusion is the business relationship was never personal, it was purely transactional (superficial). Therefore, there is certainly no reason to extend business loyalty. They will do future business wherever it is most convenient (closest), or with whom they have been most recently in contact with.

Brilliant Strategies Notebook

My thoughts on how to apply this chapter's lessons to my business...

_____

_____

_____

_____

_____

_____

_____

_____

_____

_____

_____

_____

_____

_____

_____

_____

_____

_____

_____

_____

_____

_____

"Building market dominance requires
more than developing a web site,
a fancy logo, putting a monogram
on a shirt or creating a national
ad campaign to increase
name recognition.
(Oldsmobile had name recognition)

Just because the customers know
who you are, doesn't mean they
have a reason for choosing you
over the competition."

Robert F. Krumroy

The Most Common Mistakes

COMPETING ON PRICE

Most companies that try to differentiate go about it in all the wrong ways. Lowest price is the easiest game to play, but whenever your competitor can quickly do whatever you are doing, it is a bad strategy. Anyone with deeper pockets can outlast you. Even more horrifying is the message you send – that there's nothing in your business other than price that's worthy of consideration. In such a case, loyalty is virtually nonexistent. If you attract customers with low price, they will leave you for low price.

> *Low price creates low loyalty.*

If you must use price as a differentiator, by all means make it high price. High price symbolizes quality or prestige. Just don't price your product high without giving added value. Wrap it with differentiated service, unique surroundings, or something that stands out as distinct from your competition. You may even announce boldly: "We're a great company, but you may not be able to afford to do business with us. We are not the least expensive, but we are known as excellent in what we do." It's a perception that speaks to consumers, building far more loyalty than low price.

PRODUCT BREADTH

Increasing product breadth is a dangerous, not to mention ineffective, way to differentiate your business from the competition. There invariably will be a competitor in your market who can beat you at this game. Only the giant national brand stores with their mega-buying power can use the strategy successfully. Even if you have the resources to do it, once you are "huge" because of adding product, your only point of differentiation will eventually shift back to price. And we all know where that leads.

> *You can't differentiate an "everything" store.*

It is impossible to differentiate an "everything" store. Gap stores keep their Baby Gap and teen-oriented Old Navy stores totally separate. A specialty strategy is not only easier to maintain, but it is just about the only strategy a small-business owner can effectively defend and promote. It is far more appealing and less confusing to the customer when they evaluate you, as compared to the competition.

NATIONAL AND LOCAL ADVERTISING

"What about advertising," you ask. "Won't that create customer preference? Won't that give me an advantage over the competition?" The answer is "maybe, maybe not."

Businesses may believe they have no choice but to advertise, but the kind and amount you need really depends on what you're selling. High-usage goods such as clothing, crisis-apparent services such as plumbing (yellow pages are better than TV) or frequent consumables such as groceries or fast food receive the greatest positive impact from advertising. It's why McDonald's is one of the largest advertisers in the world. Using frequent ads that tout commonplace products like copy machines, soft drinks, cars and prestige products like Rolex watches keep brands on the minds of consumers and eventually influence purchases. Some products further their brand dominance just by being part of our everyday lives, like breakfast cereal. For these, advertising makes a lot of sense.

Infrequently used products are another story. National advertising has little effect on influencing the local market if you're in the business of selling professional services or products like insurance. This is not to say that high-level national name recognition

> *National name recognition isn't the same as local market attraction.*

isn't important. Name recognition provides a certain level of comfort for clients when they're asked to write a check for the good or service, but it doesn't provide much help to the local salesperson who's trying to gain an appointment with a prospect.

An exception to the above is that high-level name recognition, achieved through advertising, does makes an impact on a company's stock price. This is because institutional investors, who buy big equity positions in a particular company, prefer buying well-known stocks. Why? Because for the person making the purchasing decision, this familiarity provides some insulation from being blamed for a bad investment choice if the stock later drops in price.

Most small-business owners, however, aren't trying to get institutional investors to purchase their stock, and many are offering products or services to the general public that are medium- or low-frequency usage products. The lower the product's usage frequency, the less impact advertising will have on attracting customers. Chances are, even money spent locally by small businesses for newspaper, TV or radio ads could be far better utilized and create a better return on investment if invested in creating a stronger *distinction intimacy*. Think about focusing efforts on becoming distinctively different and intimate to specific customers and prospects instead of trying to get the attention of the masses via the local newspaper, radio or TV.

ASSEMBLING A CUSTOMER DATABASE

Most businesses (over 50%) fail within their first year. Thereafter, seven out of every ten that survived fail within the next five years. And you can lay most of these failures at the feet of poor marketing. Additionally, chances are their business plans never addressed the issue of identifying name-specific potential customers to pursue. It's also unlikely they developed a "courting strategy" – a strategy for continuing to build preference and loyalty, even among their current clients.

> *Most failed businesses never developed a "courting strategy" to attract and keep customers.*

Businesses continue to fail because they persist in focusing on the antiquated business theory that delivering a "quality product" is sufficient. There is still precious little thought being allocated to *attraction marketing,* except for traditional media advertising. This seems particularly true for second- and third-generation family businesses and those guided by principles used by a parent/business owner in the 1960s or 1970s. Most business owners have given little or no consideration to developing a name-specific database of current customers – let alone potential customers – around which a connection strategy can be developed.

The massive lack of attention to this critical element makes you wonder whether the business owner believes that such a list – if ever needed – will somehow just appear. Many will outwardly agree that a name-specific customer database is probably critical for the future, but their inactivity certainly defines the issue as less important than their "talk" conveys, much less as a proactive objective that has garnered much of their concern.

> *Delivering a quality product is not enough.*

A new breed of business owners, the "Great Marketers," are not ignoring this issue. They are actively focused on building mindshare, by initially building databases of customer names and potential customer names. They know that the primary sale occurs first in the customer's mind, not in the store or during face-to-face selling encounters. And they know that you can't build mindshare if you don't know the names of the people you wish to influence!

> *Build a database with names of future customers you wish to influence.*

COMPANY BROCHURES

With all the information we have about what marketing is and isn't, it is almost incredible how much faith service industries still put in brochures. The reason has to be that, for years, marketing didn't have to be done.

There are scores of competitors in your market today and guess what? Most of them have the same brochures you do! Only the cover is different. Your job in the new marketing environment is not to create a new brochure but to create a brand personality that differentiates you from the competition. Marketing is not doing what everybody else is doing. Brochures may be necessary to describe a complicated process, but they are a very minor factor for creating your local image and building your local brand attraction.

One myth that seems to prevail is that brochures help in luring customers to you. But people buy YOU, not the brochure describing your product. People buy from people and businesses they like. Just as employees stay with bosses they like, your job is to create likability and constant familiarization.

> *Create likability and constant familiarization.*

If you are intent on using brochures, they need to be personalized to you, not just your company or product. Most traditional brochures promote nothing distinct. But what if your brochure promoted your differentiation and likability? Only when you know your market segment as individuals can you put together a brochure that talks about your differentiated specialty and how you personally relate to the market. Specialization elevates value perception, creates deeper appeal and gives you an easier target to influence. Annunciate that you have narrowed your market and you will automatically broaden your appeal.

The brochure that can visibly show your likability and differentiation to a specific market segment can add credibility to your image. But remember, it is still only a supporting actor. Brochures are not primary considerations for creating attraction to your business. They're not even close seconds. One final caution: Never use brochures as a mass mailing item to customers you have never met. It is an ineffective marketing technique and does nothing to endear you to a prospect.

In summary, how often have you been excited about a brochure? You probably never read them. You throw them out like old gum wrappers, paying no attention to what they say unless you already have decided that you can see yourself doing business with this person. Most brochures are validation pieces, not attraction pieces.

Remember, marketing is about creativity and innovation, not imitation. If you are going to use a brochure, make it personal. Make it distinctly different and unique from anything you have ever seen. Let it be a differentiator, not another imitation. Surprise the customer with something different.

Chapter Five

Summary Reflections

Competing for business on price is your most fatal strategy.

Low price builds no long-term customer loyalty.

Increasing product breadth ruins your business's ability to identify yourself as unique.

It is impossible to differentiate an "everything" business.

A specialty strategy is easier to promote and get recognized.

Be cautious about claims of attracting customers through media advertising (radio, TV, print). Unless your product is frequently used, is a crisis-apparent service, or is frequently consumed (car, clothing, plumbing services, food), there may be significantly better uses for your marketing (advertising) dollars. Advertising media may make sense for your type of business, but it is still never a substitute for creating a local visible distinction that attracts customers to you.

If you do advertise, don't create ads that simply explain your product or service, identify your location, or are an extension of your company's brochure. Furry animals, small children, nostalgic memories, laugh-inducing humor and strong emotion are the best advertisement surroundings for keeping the customer's attention and generating attraction. Describing your financial strength or product will stimulate a remote-control-channel-change moment almost immediately.

Build a computer database of current customers and equally important, all the name-specific potential customers you can find. Be proactive in finding names of potential customers that you can apply a connection strategy for attracting them to your business.

Brilliant Strategies Notebook

My thoughts on how to apply this chapter's lessons to my business...

"Believing you can survive the next five years without integrating technology as part of your customer connection strategy is a fatal conclusion."

Robert F. Krumroy

Chapter Six

Partnering Your Business with the Internet

To paraphrase Bill Gates, you don't have to be able to predict the future but you sure better pay attention to where it's headed. Most of us have no idea where the Internet is going. But it most definitely is going to impact the way we do business. And sooner than a lot of people probably imagine.

The traditional argument that you can't replace in-the-flesh personal contact with anything that gets the same results is too simplistic in today's marketplace and the fast approaching future. In just a few years, the Internet will be one hundred percent functionally voice-friendly, allowing everyone to take part in live, face-to-face conversations through their cable TV or computer monitor. The technology is already available for that as well as for life-like video streaming.

> *Your use of technology for customer attraction is no longer optional if you're going to survive.*

Many traditional appointments, in which the salesperson drives to a customer's home or one of you drives to the other's office, will be eliminated. Don't want your working or nonworking hours intruded on by a salesperson's visit? Meet on the Internet to talk business. To prosper, the service provider of the future will have to conduct many interviews this way. For many business owners, the change will be an opportunity; for others, a problem, one that may prove terminal. Different business owners will view it differently, but all can survive who decide to adapt.

I predict that within five to ten years we will have full Internet interactivity through cable TV, and probably with no monthly fee. When this occurs, infomercials will gain the capability to be up-close and personal with the TV audience. Want to talk with the psychic hotline? No need to call. Simply point your remote at the "Contact Us" box on the screen. The immediacy of the medium opens up limitless possibilities. Your company needs to determine NOW how to take advantage of them.

Most businesses might see the potential of the Internet primarily in terms of a product distribution channel. For the small-business owner, however, I believe the Internet's real application lies in communications. Your audience is already online. A Census Bureau survey in 2000 found that more than half of all U.S. households had computers and more than eighty percent of them had Internet access. By 2002, the number of U.S. households with minor-age children having Internet access rose to over eighty-five percent. It is estimated that over ninety percent use or check e-mail every day. Nielsen, which samples the web "universe" on a monthly basis, estimated in October 2001 that more than one hundred and sixty-nine million Americans had Internet access and averaged twenty visits a month. The statistics got a significant bump in the summer of

> *The Internet doesn't impair building personal customer relationships - it enhances them.*

2001, when Houston, Texas, launched a program to provide free e-mail and computer software to its three million residents. Similar programs are being planned for other cities.

By the year 2005, it will be as unusual to find people who are not connected to the Internet as it was to find someone in 1990 who didn't own a color television. That's why it's crucial to start collecting e-mail addresses right now. If you wait until this new age arrives, it will be too late. Your customers will have numerous opportunities to personally interact with people competing for what you thought was your business.

Go to www.my-ecustomer.com to see e-mail information packages available for small businesses.

Just last week, my credit card company called me. Unusual activity had been spotted in my account, and – "as a courtesy" – the company wanted to make sure the card had not been stolen. I confirmed that the charges were indeed mine, but the customer representative didn't hang up. She proceeded to lead me through a discussion of the company's credit card protection plan and its attractive new balance-transfer offer. Hmmm. Do you really think this all started due to a "courtesy call" to verify charges, or was this a planned and intentional cross-selling corporate strategy?

In the near future, look for courtesy calls – and follow-up "customer specialist" calls accessed by e-mail – to become commonplace. I am sure that many companies will eventually send e-mail information packages frequently to all of their clients as the company's database becomes more refined. They will use e-mail to intensify relationships and to maintain consistent emotional connection with their customer base. And the really great marketing companies will include sending information to e-mail addresses of potential customers, which they will have accumulated through numerous creative ways.

Would you like to receive an e-mail package on financial planning? Yes? More than an e-mail package, you will likely receive an interactive program that makes it easy to access specific information, provides comparisons and quotes, and gives you a message box with which to respond – or allows you to connect with a live person with whom you can chat or instant message over a chat line.

Will e-mail connection be profitable for your company? "Forget rejoicing over a two percent direct-mail response rate and start expecting something a little higher, say forty percent … that's the level of response many business-to-business e-mail marketers are experiencing." So reported a special technology article entitled "No Turning Back" in the December 1999 issue of *Sales and Marketing* magazine. With a sophisticated database that tells you when a prospect is most likely to have freed-up cash (such as a mortgage being paid off or a child finally getting out of college), response levels will be higher than ever imagined.

Database marketing will eventually affect every consumer and every line of business, and companies need to begin recognizing that. If you're going to survive, said an article in *Strategy and Business* magazine (Fourth Quarter, 1999), "The web is likely to be the center of [your] marketing future, not simply an adjunct to traditional marketing methods."

I haven't mentioned Web sites as part of the new technology you must adopt, and for a reason. A Web site provides visual proof that you are a legitimate business, and some businesses find them necessary for providing customer service. But it will not create an *Identity Brand* that differentiates you from the competition. Unless you sell a price-sensitive commodity product, it will not create any significant prospect attraction for the person who has never met you. However, e-mail will be a different issue.

> *Having a web site is hardly serious marketing. Web sites don't create initial customer attraction.*

Only businesses that adopt Internet communication technology (not Web sites) as a partner in their marketing strategies will survive. In many cases, personal contact with customers will be solely through the interactive Internet. People who want high-touch, personal relationships with service professionals or favorite stores will demand and expect technological alternatives. Time issues, business demands, privacy and convenience will require an ability to build relationships with the customer over the Internet. No excuses will remedy the loss of business you will incur if you're not in the front line of this new Internet communication race.

The following story may help you to visualize the impact of this new future.

A Story From The Future

It's a day five years from now, and Jack just got home from work. The competition on the job is more and more intense. Every company seems to want more and more out of less and less to increase their profit margins in order to stay competitive. After dinner, Jack turns on the TV and clicks on web access.

Web access, through cable TV, became a no-additional-cost

feature a couple of years ago. The speed of how it connected everyone to each other and with business has been amazing. Jack uses it all the time, for almost everything. Most people do. Especially since it is now part of everyone's cable TV. The interactive shopping channels are flourishing since it is now easy for everyone to buy nearly everything they need. Purchasing a product, or even requesting to talk to someone, only requires pointing the remote control and giving it a quick click.

Jack has agreed to be interviewed on how cable TV Internet has changed his and his family's life. Here are some excerpts from that interview.

Tell me how Internet communication has affected your family.

Well, we use it for everything now – shopping, planning vacations, buying groceries, talking to our friends, etc. It's also the first thing any of us check when we get home, kind of like how you checked your telephone answering machine years back. Wow, that's showing my age, isn't it? Now that your phone messages connect through the Internet, it's much easier to see who called before you even retrieve the message. You can prioritize how you pick them up or which ones you just discard. Even my mom and dad use it with all of their friends. It's so easy to use, especially since it's connected through the TV cable.

Can you give us some other examples of how Internet access via TV has influenced your family?

I can sure tell you that Mom, who is 76 years old, has caught on. I guess with learning to use the ATM machine at the bank, she finally figured out that her favorite show, QVC Shopping Network, wasn't any more complicated. She says that it's now even more fun to watch since she can just click and buy. I think she's addicted. She still marvels at how they merged the TV, phone and computer into one. She used to be afraid of the "computer in the box." Now, it's just part of her TV and easy to use.

What about your dad?

Oh, man, Dad thinks it's great that he can talk to a travel agent face-to-face over the TV now and plan his and Mom's next trip. (Check out www.webex.com. That service is free right now.) He planned a trip with Mom to London last year and by the time he was done communicating with the travel agent on TV, I think he had a new best friend. He even talks to his stockbroker face-to-face over the Internet now. They view stock charts together over the TV. He never really liked trading on-line but he loves talking to his broker even though each trade is nine dollars and ninety-nine cents. He's a little embarrassed when he sees his former broker at church, but that guy just never adapted to the new technology. Trekking over to his office just so they could talk face-to-face got to be too inconvenient. I mean, why travel if you can talk to someone face-to-face over the TV? And Dad hates people coming to his home to sell stuff to him. Actually, I think everyone does. Dad says his old broker always said he believed in doing business the old fashioned way and didn't think technology would ever be a serious threat. And this guy used to sell a lot of technology stocks. Figure that out – was he sleeping or what? I don't know how he's doing now – he may not still be in business though I don't think he's old enough to retire. I bet he wishes he were.

Were you surprised your parents adapted so quickly to Web TV?

Who would have guessed that the older generation would take to this like they did? I guess we never thought about the mobility issues this technology resolved or how easy it would be to use. Dad even does the grocery shopping now. He loves the virtual aisles that he wheels his virtual shopping cart down, and then the pointing and clicking. Plus, they credit his bill with all the national coupons. (Check out www.lowesfoods.com. It's available now.) I think he feels like he is in control, and he always talks to the Internet grocer, even if just to say hi. You'd think they were also best friends. Who ever thought that relationships would be easier to develop on the Internet than in person? Of course, they are communicating in person, come to think about it.

Have they bought a lot of other products or services over Web TV?

Oh, yeah! The heating and air conditioning people contact him in the spring and fall with an e-mail coupon. And the shop that changes his car's oil regularly sends him e-mail service reminders. He told me the other day that his insurance company, which is now part of a big national bank, e-mailed him recently over the TV. I think they issue his credit card, too. Anyway, I don't really know who called him – the bank, the insurance company or the credit card people – but it was a face-to-face, goodwill service contact by TV e-mail. Pretty cool! They sent him an interactive e-mail presentation through the TV on some information he could click through. He liked it and clicked on the request block to talk to a representative to answer some questions. The representative was on Web TV within seconds ...talking face-to-face! Dad really liked the guy, said he was as personable as his agent, plus it was just so convenient to talk one-to-one over the TV. He didn't even have to

leave a voice mail for the guy to get back to him. It was instanta-
neous. That is hard to beat. Don't you hate having to leave voice
mail and hope someone will call you back?

Is his insurance agent still around?

He's still around, but Dad doesn't think his agent will ever find out
he purchased an investment annuity from this e-mail TV guy. Plus,
it's just a business deal. It's not that he doesn't like him anymore;
he does. But it's not like his agent is an old college roommate or that
they see each other a lot. In fact, he barely ever hears from him.
You would think that guy would at least e-mail him once a month
with financial information, but I don't think he has ever done that.
I'm sure his national company sends him premium notices,
probably with irritating stuffers and maybe even a corporate
newsletter every so often, but that's not the same as a local contact.
Kind of makes you feel insignificant to these people. Even the local
Gap store e-mails us notices about sales nearly every month, and
our favorite local restaurant sends notifications on special events
and offers. You know, it's amazing how some small-business owners
and salespeople have just not caught on and others are so blind.
Dad told this Web TV financial representative to contact me with
information on a college fund for my twins. Dad is always trying
to help. I guess that never ends.

Did the guy call you?

Yes, and he seems really nice. I told him I already had a financial
planner and he said that was not uncommon and that it wasn't a
concern. He then asked if he could e-mail me a package I could
click through that might provide good information on college
planning.

And did he send it?

Yes, and it was great. I didn't have to go to a Web site. It just came through on my e-mail screen. It allowed me to click through five or six pages, all of which were done with animated pictures that really kept my attention. It wasn't just another online brochure with a bunch of boring words to read. I was impressed with all the information I could access so easily. (This is available now. For the financial industry, it can be seen at www.emailconcept.com. For retail and service businesses, it can be seen at www.my-ecustomer.com. The subject matter is extensive and is developed for retail and service business owners.) *He called me back about a week later and we talked over Web TV. That way we could talk face-to-face while reviewing the information together. He said most clients prefer this method. I know it sure beat having to go to his office or having him come here to the house. You know, they have got to be a great company to be this advanced.*

What about your financial planner?

My planner is a good guy, but this was really neat stuff. You know, I just don't have the time to make an appointment, as my planner always wants me to, and then meet him at his office. I wonder why my guy doesn't contact me like this. I guess most local bankers and financial advisors work pretty much the same. Not very high tech, huh? Makes you wonder if maybe the companies aren't very up-to-date either. You know, years ago I thought I would always want a personal financial advisor, but between these interactive e-mail packages and Web TV, you can't get much more personal. You know, he should really start communicating through the Internet or he could lose a lot of business, don't you think?

Why do you believe the financial service company might not be up-to-date, instead of just the financial advisor?

Well, I think it's a good company. It's big, anyway. Even so, it still doesn't have the capability to respond to questions by e-mail – in this age! Likewise, it doesn't keep me informed through an occasional e-mail newsletter or e-mail notifications about products, updates or anything. Even the airlines, clothing stores and car rental companies do that! Sure, the company has a Web site, but that's not exactly a place you go back to visit. You know, I bet they don't even have their clients' e-mail addresses. They certainly have never asked for mine. I mean, even my church has done that and uses it to send me weekly announcements. How hard is this? Everyone's e-mail address has been in an Internet directory for four years now. (Check out www.switchboard.com.) And forget about their getting plugged into this Web TV thing. How can a company be so far behind? It really makes you wonder about their products and everything. If I were the financial advisor, I'd find a different company. Or maybe it's me who should find a different financial planner.

Well, I can't help you there. Tell me what else your dad liked about the Web TV bank representative he spoke with?

He invited Dad to an investment presentation with a big investment company. They do that every quarter. He will love that, and who knows – maybe I'll go with him. They also have a live Web TV conference each week for local clients to tune into. Kind of neat when you have an investment hour each week on the stocks and mutual funds you own.

What would your financial planner say if he knew you were going with your dad to the investment presentation?

He would probably be upset. On the other hand, he probably would never find out. I wonder how he's doing now with the banks, CPAs and everyone doing the same thing. The competition in every area is really fierce. Plus, now with Web TV ... well, Dad really likes that convenience and I do, too. This new relationship-building on Web TV, being able to deal with people face-to-face and not leave your home, is just too easy for people not to get involved with it.

Why else do you sense your agent might be having a hard time?

Well, selling an intangible product is pretty hard. The products are virtually the same with all companies. At least I can't see a difference. It's not like a car, where something is visibly distinct and it's something you just have to have. I know that every company has its own little differences, but common sense tells you that the products are fairly equal. I guess it's not really the product you're buying anymore; it's the experience you have with the local business and what they provide other than the product. The little extra things they do for you, like the wine-tasting investment events they invite you to, etc. I don't mean the selling experience, but the ongoing experience kind of stuff.

You said you thought it was probably harder to sell financial products today. Why?

Now that the banks and everyone else are contacting people directly, it has really gotten tough. They can also offer big investment events now and there are Web TV weekly reviews that keep you up to date. Did I tell you that a specialty "cruise only" travel company is co-sponsoring this next investment event with a special presentation about the Greek Islands? There's going to be a wine tasting at the end of the evening. That sure grabs your attention – I can even get my wife to go to something like that! It makes the event more like an entertainment evening instead of a typical boring seminar. That's the type of experience stuff I'm talking about. It's different from the same-old, same-old. That's the stuff that attracts and keeps customers.

Does your financial planner offer anything like this?

No, and I can't figure that out. It's got to be tough just to get people to notice you, and he does nothing that makes himself stand out or be more likable than the competition. He's probably a good planner ... but aren't they all about the same? They all look alike, a bunch of Me-Too financial advisors, except for this guy who does these unique things. He must be different, don't you think?

Why do you think your financial planner doesn't spend more time trying to do at least some things like this? You would think his company would help him.

I think he's just trying to survive. I don't see him often and don't hear from him often either – maybe a birthday card, but that's hardly unique. My hairdresser and my mechanic both send me birthday cards. My planner's company sends me some mailings, but that's not the same. I don't know why he didn't get involved with this new technology. Do you think he just didn't see it coming? His company should have helped him, but maybe they're the one's holding him back. But he shouldn't have waited. He just should have gotten involved somehow. I'm sure he's lost a lot of business – and a lot of clients.

Chapter Six

Summary Reflections

Technology is no longer optional. It must become part of every business's customer connection strategy. Now is the time to get Internet savvy. Waiting has nothing but inferior or negative outcomes.

Internet access for families with children between 4 and 17 years old is reported to be as high as 85%, with daily e-mail access exceeding 90%. Senior connection is the fastest growing segment in America.

Internet communication will be a critical component for your business survival.

Ask for e-mail addresses and build an e-mail database.

Creating a Web site is not a substitute for developing a strategy of proactive e-mail communication that adds value to the recipient's life.

You must figure out a way to frequently initiate a connection with your name-specific target audience.

Brilliant Strategies Notebook

My thoughts on how to apply this chapter's lessons to my business...

_____

_____

_____

_____

_____

_____

_____

_____

_____

_____

_____

_____

_____

_____

_____

_____

_____

_____

_____

_____

_____

_____

_____

"The driving force for attaining market dominance is not product. It is creativity. Differentiation."

Robert F. Krumroy

Chapter Seven

Clutter-Breaking the Consumer's Mind

Today's world is so full of media stimulation, advertising and product hype that most people have retracted their mental antennas, turned off their listening mechanisms and desensitized their very beings to an almost voluntary comatose state. If we could use the TV remote for just one purpose, I daresay most people would choose it to eliminate commercials. The general population is frustrated. No, we're more than frustrated, we're irritated. The barrage of everybody's claims is too much to tolerate. And we certainly don't welcome more.

Getting attention today requires doing something to break through the clutter. The traditional business plan would have you spending laborious time developing logos and brochures. But these exercises are so far removed from success requirements for the typical American small business that it seems almost foolish to comment on them.

Somehow, you must break through the noise and clutter to attract attention.

Businesses that still see product as the primary customer lure have missed the message the consumer is sending. "Most customers today ... are deeply unimpressed by isolated benefits offered by faceless products and hard-sell advertising of the problem/solution type," Schmitt and Simonson argue in *Marketing Aesthetics*. "We are awash in high-quality look alike/me-too products and services...The customer of today makes choices based on a desirable experience." If you are still living in the 1970s belief that product benefits will give you "the edge," you are going to be quickly outdistanced by the new generation of "Great Marketers," those who are learning to sell the experience and then maintain consistent emotional connections. These are today's great selling points.

Yesterday, service marketers believed that prospecting and selling were their most important skills. Today, great marketers know that the most important skill is launching their differentiated business image to a specific audience and getting prospects to genuinely want to connect.

> *Brands today are far more than a product.*

Brands today are far more than the composite elements that make up a product. As we have said before, success has very little to do with product quality, benefits, features or advantages. Your logo and company name may be clever, your brochure dazzling, but the bombardment of advertising stimuli has rendered the average consumer nearly comatose. Traditional advertising may still help in building brand name recognition, but that doesn't translate into local business attraction. The marketing staples of yesterday simply fail to deliver the spellbinding effects they may have done in the 1970s.

Neither have brands become dominant products as the result of the typical cost/benefit sales approach, even though it's still regarded by many businesses as the primary way to sell their products. Many continue to believe that delivering better sales training or a "refresher course" to salespeople will improve their results. They are wrong. Most of your sales people don't have a selling problem. Assuming you have an effective sales program, refreshing your staff's skills isn't going to drastically improve anything.

Aesthetic considerations like packaging, store layout, product display and spatial planning do make a difference. However, their impact is far greater when the strategy is planned as part of the dynamic and ongoing process of building an "experience." The point is to increase consumer mindshare and business preference and to continue to differentiate your business from the competition. This process can never end and neither can it remain static. It must always be revisited, constantly changed and updated as the consumer changes. It seems so simple, but it isn't easy. It is particularly easy to lose your focus on the critical element of differentiation while concentrating on product, financial and employee issues.

> *Building the customer's "experience" needs to be a never-ending objective*

Gap® is a great example. The retail clothing chain had both its ups and downs as a fashion store during the 1990s. Then from about 1997 to early 2000, it was all up. It seemed the company could do no wrong. Its stock price rocketed; every investor wanted a piece of the Gap! Eventually, though, something did go wrong. Gap's stock changed direction and by mid-2000, plummeted. All the while, analysts continued to predict a comeback. (As of this writing, that has not happened.) In November 2000, an Associated Press article termed the Gap's problems "an identity crisis" and quoted analysts as citing "too many varied looks" for the downturn in its fortunes.

Too many varied looks? But isn't that a strategy that attracts the greatest number of customers. More is better, right? Well, obviously not. In its earlier days, Gap goods had a distinctive look. But eventually what they were selling started looking like everybody else's, and any store that continues to add product eventually becomes undifferentiated. We have said before that you can't differentiate an "everything store." Differentiation requires keeping a distinctively narrow focus, especially for the small-business owner.

> *Without "differentiating" your business, you are going to fail.*

The point is: Differentiation is not optional. Without it, you are going to fail. And when it begins to fade, you are going to feel the effect. Regardless of your logo, your company name, your flashy brochures or your Web sites, when your differentiation becomes blurred, you have a serious problem. And it will be fatal if not corrected quickly.

Now for some inspiration! The following segments of this chapter are dedicated to small local businesses that have captured an emotional bond with their customers. Their stories are all different but they all contain this common strategy: to be visibly differentiated, to make frequent connection, to stand out as distinctive and intensify relationships within their market, in order to create an irresistible appeal, a compelling association between their business and the local consumer. And remember, your business, any business, can do this as well.

Classic Import Service

Bob and Mary Heybrock own a very high-level auto repair shop, one that services only Mercedes, Jaguars and Volvos. I don't know how many people in the local community who own one of those automobiles go to Bob and Mary, but it's a lot. Their special focus on high-level automobiles, however, is not what differentiates Classic Import Service of Greensboro, North Carolina. It is Bob and Mary who have implemented all three components necessary to become a local market brand: building a name-specific database, creating market intrigue (differentiation) and maintaining consistent connection. Here is the story of how they have done it, and it will give you new respect for the power of doughnuts.

A visit to Classic Import Service is akin to entering a friend's home. Bob and Mary make a point of personally introducing customers to one another and to the staff. No one is left in the reception area feeling like a stranger. The shop also lacks the traditional counter and glass window. When you come to drop off your car, you're escorted into Bob's office, where he or Mary writes up your service order. When you come back to pick up the car, you can expect to get a big hug from Mary and a big smile from Bob.

The sweetness doesn't end there. Every Thursday at Classic Import is "Doughnut Day." They make such a big deal about getting a free doughnut that Thursday has become a preference day that established customers knowingly request. It's one of those elements that add a humanizing touch-point to an impersonal product, an almost corny likability to a business that inevitably must present customers with a bill. And that is what branding is all about.

... add a humanizing touch-point

That's not all they do. Before taking off on vacations twice a year, the Heybrocks send out mailings that weave together their personal connection to customers with essential business information. There's chat about their travel itinerary ("wish you were going with us") and the dates the shop will be closed. They stress the importance of scheduling needed service around those dates, with Mary adroitly adding humor to drive the point home. In one such mailing, she said Bob was complaining that the vacation would be expensive and she might have to limit her shopping. "Bob would shoot me if he knew I mentioned that, but if you can please get your car serviced, not only would you and your car be happier but I will have a better chance of getting an extra shopping day in." The cards always end with a plug for Doughnut Day.

I'm a big fan of these mailings. The personal messages make me smile just to think of them. Now that's likability! These are real people who provide memorable experiences on a consistent basis, and their customers feel they know them personally.

> *... provide memorable experiences*

Remember that old Ma Bell commercial? It showed a grandmotherly woman on the front porch of her farmhouse receiving a call from her grown businessman son? It was guaranteed to put a tear in your eye. We experienced that same lump-in-the-throat feeling from the 1980s commercial that showed a weary, hobbling "Mean" Joe Green tossing his football jersey to a young fan who gave him a bottle of Coke.

Do you remember more about the goods and services in those commercials or the humanizing touch-point? Customers are more attracted to the experience they are purchasing today than the product attached to it. They are looking for connection, and Bob and Mary Heybrock are the role models for making their customers feel connected.

Classic Import Service. is celebrating 11 years of business!

We want to thank you for being part of our business and a part of our success. With your continued business and referrals, we will continue to move forward.

Thank you again!

Sincerely,

Bob, Mary & George

For Valentine's Day, they send out a special note that not only shows personal appreciation for customers but also encourages continued loyalty. They include in the mailing a pink, heart-shaped card on which customers are encouraged to write a testimonial about "what they love" about Classic Import Service. The returned cards are displayed in the shop's reception area, and the creator of the message judged the best is rewarded with a free oil change. Bob and Mary also send out special holiday mailings for Thanksgiving Day and the Fourth of July, and in addition every customer receives a personally inscribed birthday card.

Surprise and delight your customers.

Be My Valentine!

February is the "love" month. We want our clients to know how much we love them so for the month of February, stop by and pick up a flower for your sweetie or if you just need one for yourself! If you have your car worked on, pull a heart from the "money" tree for a coupon. There will be a couple of surprises from Cupid.

Again, we thank all of you for your continued business and for helping us celebrate 10 years in this community.

Sincerely,

Bob & Mary Heybrock

Classic
Import
Service, Inc.
854-1001

CLASSIC IMPORT SERVICE, INC.
129 MANLEY AVENU
GREENSBORO NC 27407
336-854-1001

February is a month for love. Classic Import Service wants you, our faithful clients to know we appreciate your business.

Use the heart attached to write your name, address and a brief description of what you like about our company. Bring it or mail it back and we will display this heart on a board in our lobby. At the end of the month, a dart will be thrown (arrow if you will) and 3 participants will win an $80.00 valued clean-up certificate for their car.

Everyone else that returned their heart will have a $10.00 coupon on the board when they come in. Pull it off and give it to the cashier as you check out.

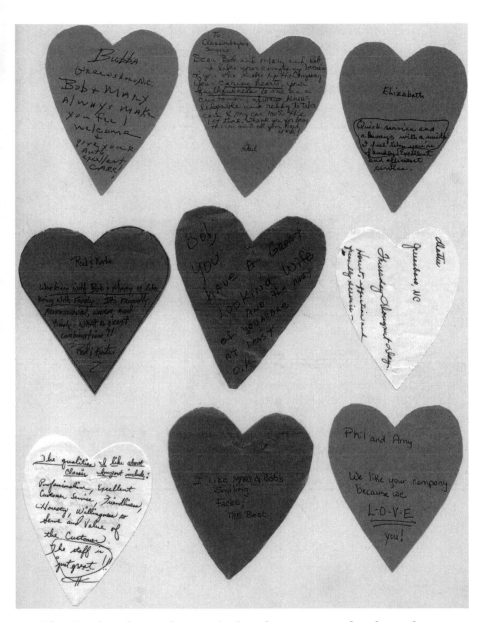

The Heybrocks understand that becoming a local market identity brand is a two-way street. It's important to know your customer, and it's equally important for your customer to know you. These successful business owners stay focused on surprising and delighting their clients, by showing their human side in addition to providing quality products and services. They understand that people crave appreciation and that it is most noticed when expressed in unique ways. The result is an incredibly loyal customer base – people who believe their lives (not just their cars!) are better because of their friends, Bob and Mary. The Heybrocks have mastered the concept of selling the experience.

It's amazing how many service businesses provide a quality service but then don't keep in consistent touch with past customers. By just occasionally sending out a product promotion announcement – nothing particularly personal, creative or memorable – they're missing out on a simple and profitable way to gain repeat business. Giving quality service is not a differentiator – not by itself. Past customers do business with those that are on their mind when they need someone, businesses that create and maintain an emotional bond. That's why creating market intrigue and likability through making consistent connections has to be a never-ending effort. It can also be fun and cost very little money.

No-Name Soup Kitchen

I hear a lot of reasons why people feel it's impossible to differentiate their business. They all have something in common. They're all stuck in the "Me-Too" mold, and that's the kiss of death as far as stellar growth is concerned.

Great marketing demands that you find a way to surprise and delight the customer. It doesn't have to cost a lot, but it does require unconventional thinking. You must figure out how to do two things: look differentiated and develop a strategy to frequently connect with the people you specifically want to do more business with.

> *You must frequently connect with your customers and prospects.*

Frequent connection with customers and prospects is an absolute necessity. When connections are infrequent, the relationship quickly becomes depersonalized and superficial – and that's not a good foundation for building and maintaining a sustainable emotional bond with your prospects and customers.

Consider the No-Name Soup Kitchen in Chicago (another in Roanoke, VA), which serves nothing but soup and fresh baked rolls. The small restaurant, which is primarily takeout due to having space for just half a dozen tables, is only open for lunch Monday through Friday. Every year since opening, the eatery has enjoyed booming business, and one of the reasons undoubtedly must be that the owners know how to give the customer a memorable experience.

There's always a line, but service is extraordinarily efficient. Regulars take getting barked at by staff as part of the fun. When you get to the front, a chalkboard tells which eight soups are offered on that particular day. The soup names are smile-inducing, the likes of "Mama's Axe-Killing Potato Soup," "Take Your Last Breath Chili," or "Chicken Little's Barnyard Noodle Ecstasy."

The staff is incredibly good at spotting first-time customers, singling them out for a hearty spiel about how wonderful the soups are ("the best of your life!"). They offer a free Momma's Bunn (a huge yeast roll) in exchange for filling out a registration card. "Give us your name, birthday and e-mail address so we can stay in touch. Be quick! There are other customers behind you who will kill you if you take too long deciding. Plus, Momma may not be too happy either if you take too long thinking about your answer." Everyone in line smiles; they've all been through this experience.

The No-Name Soup Kitchen is serious about those registration cards. For the rest of their lives, customers are going to receive a personal e-mail message at least twice a week announcing the soups of the week, the weather forecast for Chicago, and even a mention or two about family matters, such as the staff's children's math test results. It's a strategy that creates likability and humanizes the business. Local businesspeople can't easily forget this place for lunch, and even out-of-towners are likely to spread the word.

> *What do you do that creates "likability"?*

Consumers always give preference to businesses that are most frequently on their minds. But print advertising is not the be-all and end-all answer in an overcrowded marketplace. Attracting and keeping customers requires personally touching their hearts on a regular basis.

You might be surprised how inexpensive it would be to adapt

this idea to your business. Get an e-mail address, develop a strategy to meaningfully connect with customers and then make that connection at least eight times a year. There are even e-mail providers now (www.my-ecustomer.com is one example) that specialize in working with small businesses and professionals to provide distinctive marketing messages.

How many restaurants, retail businesses, professionals or service providers have you done business with and never heard from again? Or maybe you do hear from them but only with the typical yearly birthday card or holiday greeting card. It's no wonder research shows that seventy percent of potential repeat business goes elsewhere, not back to the original vendor they did business with.

Contacting your customers once or twice a year is simply not enough to win their affection, much less their deep loyalty. And just because you have a retail business with good product selection and prices, it doesn't mean your customers will return simply because their last encounter was satisfying. A

> *A satisfied customer is not enough.*

satisfied customer is not enough. With all the new competition, you need to strategize creative ways to stay on their mind.

What strategy are you using to deepen customer loyalty; to create an emotional bond and to build your personal business image? In business, familiarity does not breed contempt – non-familiarity does! Mindshare is initiated through providing memorable experiences, thereafter it must be forever nurtured for a business to develop its full potential as a dominate market brand. Just look at the No-Name Soup Kitchen's success. No one does it better.

Tobacco USA

Jerry Pappas emerged from World War II with a dream of going into business for himself. Starting with little money but with the full support of his family and his own big heart, Pappas grew Tobacco USA, in Greensboro, NC, into a notable presence in the community.

For its first twenty-five years, Jerry's tobacco wholesale company experienced and survived all the pain and challenges of surviving. In 1971, however, the marketplace was about to change. Now a seasoned and savvy business owner, he sensed the winds of change and was ready to react, if only he could determine the right response. Better operational efficiency would not be the answer this time. Survival would require adaptation, a new strategy, possibly a complete redefining of his business.

> **Better operational efficiency is not marketing.**

In 1972, he made his move, opening Tobacco USA to the public and offering retail customers the cost savings previously given just bulk purchasers. He also expanded into paper goods. At the time, Kmart and Wal-Mart were making a major impact with their strategy of price attraction, and Jerry felt he could still compete if he strategized a critical difference. That difference was not to increase product breadth but to intentionally accentuate his business's narrow focus. His focus on tobacco and paper products created a perception of "specialty" versus being just another product/price competitor.

He was ahead of his time. Maintaining a narrow product offering would later surface as a strong strategy for retailers, as you can see with Gap for Kids, Victoria's Secret and

Starbuck's Coffee, to name but a few. And with this new strategy in place, Tobacco USA enjoyed a growing customer base.

It wasn't long, however, before Jerry was forced yet again to chart a new course for his business. By the mid-1970s, he had drifted into the all-too-common trap of continuing to increase product offerings. The store now offered tobacco products, paper goods, candy, groceries and snacks. Though still

> *Increasing your product breadth is a dangerous strategy.*

known as a wholesale price store, the business was going downhill. Increasing the product selection, ever so slowly over the years, had eroded its differentiation. Now seen by shoppers as a "Me-Too" business, Tobacco USA was subject to having its prices compared to the larger discount stores or any other competitors with similar merchandise breadth.

Jerry Pappas' survival instinct and competitive spirit began to stir. Sons Matthew and Jerome were now in business with him, and he posed the challenge to them. It went along these lines: "We can't afford to be like other stores. We can't compete with price or product breadth. To survive, we have to be different." Being "different" became their rallying cry, and it continues to permeate their business strategy today.

By the early 1980s, Tobacco USA had re-created itself into a specialty store focused on party products, house wares and cookware. It continued to evolve, but always with a focus on only adding products that were not available in other stores. By the mid-'80s, the store became especially noted for its selection of gourmet foods, condiments, imported foods, boutique wines, imported beer, high-end and unusual house wares and cookware. Tobacco USA became a one-of-a-kind store that no longer needed to compete on price.

Jerry's lesson to his sons, always pursue what is different, was learned well. In 1988, the brothers added a coffee roaster to the store, the first in the local market. Not only did they see an opportunity to be first but also to be uniquely noticed and differentiated. Their vision was to impact the public as much as it was to create another profit channel.

Always pursue what is different.

They installed the roaster, a piece of equipment the size of a car, in the middle of the store, where a full-time coffee specialist kept it actively functioning, creating customer intrigue. This resident roaster was also present to answer questions and help customers customize special blends. The Pappas brothers didn't stop there. They sold area restaurants on the idea of creating signature blends of freshly roasted coffee as a way to create their own distinction in the growing restaurant industry. The restaurants were delighted and so were their patrons, who were inevitably led to make their own visits to Tobacco USA.

In the intervening years, Matthew and Jerome have carefully maintained their store's differentiation, regularly monitoring what the competition sells, ridding their store of products offered elsewhere, aiming to always maintain product exclusivity.

In 1997, they came up with yet another brilliant idea to enhance customer and community attraction: a coffee club. Buy ten pounds of coffee and the next pound is free. Coffee customers were also signed up for a new quarterly newsletter called *The Coffee Scoop*. Almost immediately there was an upsurge in repeat business, spurring Matthew to propose a quarterly wine newsletter. That was also a success. Before long there was a cooking newsletter (the store had started offering gourmet-cooking classes) and then a cigar newsletter.

Buy anything at Tobacco USA today and you stand a good chance of getting on a newsletter distribution list, along with more than nine thousand other customers. Matthew Pappas is a true-blue believer in the need for constant familiarization. "You have to keep it in their heads...all that you offer," he says. "And you have to do it often." In that vein, the store plans to double its newsletter production schedule to eight times a year. (The one-page newsletters are designed and

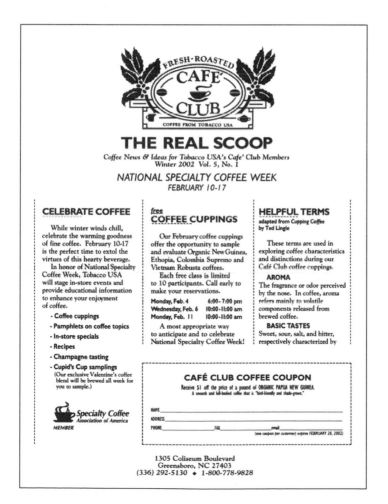

> *You have to stay on your customer's mind.*

produced by a professional writer and the cost is nominal, less than one hundred dollars per issue.)

Watch for Matthew Pappas and the Tobacco USA sign when you see community projects as well. They regularly participate in a coffee sampling table at the Symphony Orchestra Guild's annual Tour of Homes show. They also have started offering free cooking classes during the three days of the tour, another way to get noticed and make a connection with the public. Likewise, you'll see them handing out free coffee at fundraisers for Habitat for Humanity and the local Triad Health Project, among others. If you see them, don't forget to fill out a coupon card at their tables – name, address and e-mail address. They always offer that opportunity, along with a little friendly coaxing when you get your cup of coffee. Not only will you get something for free, or at a deep discount, but they will have captured your name for a newsletter or an e-mail announcement.

The marketing culture that Jerry Pappas passed along to his sons today embraces the entire Tobacco USA workforce. Matthew meets with the eighteen employees four times a year to seek ideas on building customer loyalty, making improvements and gathering feedback about products and service. He also asks employees in each department to provide ideas for the newsletters. The business is rewarded with outstanding employee loyalty. Twelve of the eighteen have worked there for more than five years.

As for the e-mail addresses they collect, Matthew isn't sure exactly what they will ultimately do with them. But like his father, a visionary is always ready to act on the next opportunity, and always before the competition has even thought about it.

Paradise Decking

When the economy went south in the early 1990s, sinking his Long Island, New York, home renovation company, Larry Knight found that his salvation lay in heading south himself.

He had started Larry Knight Carpentry and Alterations right out of college in 1973. The Long Island area was ripe for renovations. Initially, there was very little new construction since vacant land was in short supply. But the area's old homes, though charming, had hit their maturity threshold. The homes needed renovation and the owners needed renovators. The work was plentiful, and a new entrant into renovation work could easily be accommodated. But, twenty years later that story was going to change.

By 1992, construction was nose-diving in the Long Island area. The economy had bottomed. People were being

> *When you narrow your focus, you always increase your appeal.*

displaced from jobs they had held for years, and families were uprooted. Larry quickly found out that the slumping economy was not going to leave him unaffected. Eventually, the bills that others owed him for completed renovation work to their homes were going to go unpaid.

Finally, in 1993, Larry Knight had enough. He felt that in order to stay in his field of work, he had to leave Long Island. He had lost his home, work was scarce, if non-existent, and he had already waited too long. With less than fifteen hundred dollars left to his name, Larry moved his wife and two children to an area where the economy was still strong and work was available: Greensboro, North Carolina.

They moved into an apartment, and Larry began talking to local construction companies. Though he was offered a job, the resounding question that everyone asked him was, "Why don't you go out on your own, start your own company?" He was obviously qualified, but no one knew the whole story. Like a prizefighter who had been normally stronger and more talented than most of his challengers, Larry had been beaten. He was bruised and stunned, but not out. With an act of courage, Larry stood back up and entered the ring, one more time. But this time, it was going to be different.

Larry's creative side in design had always been his strength, and going to art school for college had proven to be a tremendous complement to his natural ability in construction. Now, as he was deciding what to do next, a former professor's words came back to him: "When you become really satisfied with what you're doing, that's when you'll level off." Suddenly he understood what Professor Gilbert Stone meant. Years of general carpentry had left him stifled. If he was starting over, Larry wanted to specialize in something where he could get better and better, while continuing to refine his artistic expression. Creative design was his ultimate goal. No more bathroom renovations or putting kitchens in. With a certain amount of skill, he felt like anyone could do that. Larry wanted more.

He renamed his company Paradise Decking, specializing in the design and construction of creative decks and screened porches. He was determined for it to become the premier company of its kind in the area. He would never compromise his focus, not even when the customer would ask if he wanted the additional work since they were already on location.

This new beginning wasn't easy. There was little money and little time to survive a slow start. Larry printed up flyers and tacked them on mailboxes. He picked neighborhoods where he felt residents might want a deck and could afford his work. He went to upper- income shopping centers and placed flyers on car windows and posted signs on phone polls. His flyers proclaimed Paradise Decking as "the deck specialists."

Larry had accomplished, though accidentally, what a good market consultant would have advised. He strategically determined what his market distinction was going to be and then he accentuated and boldly proclaimed his differentiation to a specific audience. By narrowing his focus, he broadened his appeal. His strategy had worked. People noticed and called. He was on his way, once again.

Accentuate and boldly proclaim your differentiation to a specific audience.

Only six years later, Larry rebuilt his dream house again – six thousand feet of artistic expression, a home whose beauty and craftsmanship are enviable. Larry's business has grown more than twenty percent per year. He keeps three construction crews busy and spends most of his time designing and creating.

Larry still uses three primary methods for attracting new business – distributing flyers on cars and mailboxes (not in the newspaper!), placing signs in strategic places (today he has more than two hundred displayed) and obtaining referrals from happy customers.

> *Media advertising a non-frequently-used product will never yield much of a result.*

Newspaper advertising was tried, but yielded dismal results, an outcome we could have forecasted. Advertising a non-consumable, non-frequently-used product in the newspaper will never yield much of a result. It is a common marketing mistake most service businesses make and usually the most ineffective use of marketing money they can spend.

On the other hand, unlike the result for most service providers, yellow pages have been productive enough for Larry to continue. The reason? The fewer businesses in your category and the narrower your specialty, the greater the chance for success in the yellow pages. Larry has only five other businesses in his category within the yellow page listings. If you're a service provider and have more than ten competitors advertising in the yellow pages, don't spend your money in this medium – even if you can afford the biggest ad. The only exception is if you are a "crisis apparent" service provider such as a plumber. When a crisis hits that is self-apparent, the yellow pages are a solution-seeker's resource.

A final disappointment Larry expresses are the minimal

results he received from participating in the annual Home Show at the local coliseum. He found the show yielded very little in comparison to the effort and expense involved. Again, it's a familiar sentiment expressed by many veterans, who eventually discover that a large general trade show audience is poorly focused, generally attracts lots of wishful browsers, and the clutter of noise is more confusing than helpful.

What else did Larry do to attract business? He intentionally targeted (didn't just wait around and hope it would happen) and then cultivated an alliance with what most people would consider to be the largest and highest quality spa dealer in Greensboro, Catalina Spa. This fusion marketing effort has worked well for both businesses.

With a little creative thinking and effort, every business owner has a strategic alliance opportunity they could cultivate that would be profitable for both parties. Larry makes sure he stays in touch with his alliance partner on a regular basis; he never allows the relationship to go cold. They both bring the highest quality products to the client and the highest level of customer concern to every job.

> *Every business owner has a strategic alliance opportunity waiting to be cultivated.*

People who contract with Larry for a deck or screened-in porch consistently remark on his practice of calling them at least three evenings every week, if not every night during a two- to three-week job. He calls just to ask if you're happy with the progress and if there is anything that needs to be done differently.

How many contractors have ever called you to enquire about your happiness? Most of the time, you're just happy if they show up. Larry's personal code of ethics is to call the customer at least three times per week, show up every day at each site (another novel idea that contractors could adopt), do a quality job and clean up every day like it was his own home. Not a speck of construction debris is to be left on the job. Larry has won a permanent place in his many customers' heart. They all hope this former Yankee is here to stay.

Diamond Oil Company

Jason Chance had no intention of taking over the family business. The CPA had been with Deloitte & Touche in Houston, Texas, for seven years when he got a call for help from his dad in 1998. No, he definitely was not interested in becoming a small business owner, but he would come home to Des Moines, Iowa, to evaluate the books and help get a good price for the company.

The Diamond Oil Co. had opened its doors in 1978 when Jason's father purchased a distribution site from Sunoco Oil. The next year, Sunoco offered the new company a local distribution contract for racing fuels. Jason's father snapped up the rights – even though he had little idea of what to do with them. At the time, there were no racing customers and apparently no business structure that could provide guidance on how to find or attract customers. This part of the business would need to be built from scratch.

Diamond Oil progressed and grew in the early years, probably more from demand than by design. In the 1980s and early 1990s, just having the products was fifty percent of the cause for market demand because dealers had few choices in distributors. By 1998, however, numerous competitors had taken their place in the business landscape, and suddenly the future looked more questionable.

After arriving home, it didn't take long for Jason to have a change of heart about the business. Maybe it just got into his blood, as it had for his dad. He began thinking in terms of salvaging and growing the business, not selling it. The challenge had become personal.

The original business plan had been loosely defined,

> *Most business plans are loosely defined, if defined at all.*

depending largely on supply and demand. Jason's father focused the monthly objective on selling large bulk quantities of fuel, usually eight thousand gallons at a time. The strategy had been to wait for customers to call, which is how most distributors still operate today. Shrewdly, Jason quickly pinpointed that here was where the company needed to change, and fast.

After talking with customers, one of Jason's first initiatives was to start a "milk run" to regularly deliver fifty-five-gallon drums of race fuel to smaller subset dealers. Today, more than fifty dealers are on the route, receiving new supplies every one to three weeks. In emergencies, they can count on Diamond Oil to respond within forty-eight hours.

The milk run strategy has now been adopted by many Sunoco race fuel distributors, but Jason was able to claim it as a differentiator because he was first. It has made him a "standout" performer; capturing mindshare within his territory of race fuel dealers.

Distinctively different from most distributors, Jason no longer waits for potential customers to recognize their need and call in an order. He calls them the week before the milk run hits their area. Every customer is called at least every three weeks – many every two weeks! And prospects, people he has identified and would like to have as active customers, are called at least once a month. "Things have a way of changing," he says, "and I want to be in place as their second-favorite supplier for the day when their first supplier stumbles." One of his favorite sayings is: "The water rushing against the rock eventually wears the rock away."

That saying appears to have substance. Jason believes that the frequency of a connection does, in fact, determine the depth of one's preference within the market. His frequent connection strategy is capturing new customers as well as continuing to build deeper preference and loyalty among existing customers.

Jason believes that you can no longer wait for the customer to identify their own needs; you have to focus on anticipating needs. "Spoon feed" the customer, even though they are adults. Initiate the communication, instead of waiting for them to call you. And learn to connect on more than just the product level. If the only time you connect with a customer is when your hands are reaching into their pockets, you're not going to be welcomed into their lives as an invaluable business partner. And that's dangerous in an overcrowded marketplace of competitors – where loyalty can shift very quickly.

"The water rushing against the rock eventually wears the rock away." (referring to consistently connecting with potential customers.

On-going pro-active customer communication is vital.

Groom Industries

I meet and talk with a lot of business owners in my travels around the country. I've heard a lot of stories, sometimes upbeat and sometimes desperate, and they reveal a commonality among those who are doing the best. These successful executives tell me they personally make sure their business is continually perceived as unique, distinct and likable. They wouldn't even consider delegating this important job.

Whenever I think of likability, Frank Beach pops into my mind. He is president and CEO of Groom Industries in Rockford, Illinois. The company is quite successful, with its Perky Carpet Care product on the shelves at Home Depot. Even so, Beach is no more distant from the customer than when he started his business more than eighteen years ago.

Asked what he considers his most important job, he will surprise you. "I personally telephone as many of our top customers every month as possible - sometimes as many as forty." How in the world does a top executive find the time to do that? He responds: "What can you think of that would be more important than talking to our top customers every month?"

You couldn't precisely call them sales calls, he says, because they're all personal friends. "Sometimes I call to just say hello, to wish them happy birthday. I always ask about their families, their vacation plans and lots of personal things that I make notes about, not just for business reasons but because I care. I probably talk to them about product maybe four times a year. It seems like a lot of product orders just naturally happen." And what about his sales staff? "Oh, they do the same thing," he says. "They personally contact the other customers each month."

> *"I personally telephone our top forty customers every month."*
> *- Frank Beach, President*

I can't help but reflect on a friend's twenty-plus years in sales and marketing at a national company. He had been their number-one or number-two manager for a decade. He had chaired top committees, produced national training films and built the company's largest production office. At one time, he even interviewed for the position of national vice president. And yet over the last five years, while the company was focusing on going public, he never received a single call from a senior person in the home office just to say "Hello" or "Good job!" The only calls he received concerned either so-called "minor problems" that had surfaced with people in the organization or budget-reduction requests for annual planning. The result? You guess. At 50 years old and 23 years of stellar performance, he resigned.

How many sales managers do you know who constantly lose their sales people? Or managers who complain about how

Do you call your top customers once a month? Once a quarter? What's more important?

little loyalty there is with their sales organizations or customers today. Or business owners who are incensed about losing one of their big accounts, especially after all the quality service and favors they have extended over the years. Yet how many of these owners, salespeople and managers ever called their top customers or top sales people each month ... each quarter ... or even once a year to just say thanks, to extend themselves in friendship and genuine sincerity.

What a difference it would make in their companies and with their customers. It may require creating a planned strategy, but as Frank Beach would say, "what could possibly be more important?"

Johnson Retirement
and Investment Specialists

Most local service providers and professionals, people like chiropractors, CPAs, lawyers or insurance firms, all look the same. They have spent so many years focusing on product, service and advanced training that they usually overlook how to attract prospects. They essentially do nothing that makes them appear any different from anyone else in their field. They believe that by simply gaining experience and technical expertise, they will be noticed and their business will grow. It's a faulty conclusion. When someone finally does differentiate himself or herself, they win big. And at your expense.

> *Most professionals all look the same ... and it's not very exciting.*

Assuming that you provide a quality service in your profession, your next higher level of success is more dependent on creating a powerful attraction toward you than it is about trying to outdo the competition by convincing your customer that you provide a slightly higher quality service or product. Your attraction focus should be more directed to determining what you can do to have a positive effect on the texture of life for the people you are connecting with than about trying to convince them that you have product superiority or a higher knowledge level within your field.

The success level you reach will be highly dependent on getting yourself noticed, due to the differentiated experience people get if they choose to do business with you. Keep in mind that if you look relatively the same as your competitors, you will lose. People want more than service providers who look relatively the same. Sameness provides no attraction power. What captured your attention when you think of your past? The answer is unique experiences. They make an indelible impression. What is it that you offer that is different than your competition?

> *Sameness provides no attraction power.*

Here's the story of a service provider who answered that question. Certified Financial Planner Jack Johnson had been a sales agent for some years in the financial services industry. Too many years, he might say. He worked hard, provided quality service and was generally regarded as very successful. But he had come to a crossroads. His motivation and personal satisfaction were dwindling fast, and in 1990 he decided that he had to reinvent his career.

One of the critical decisions Jack made was to narrow his market to people over fifty-five, an age group he felt an affinity for and believed he could serve well. He began a monthly two-hour retirement and asset-protection luncheon seminar. The program covers a dozen issues, and before making his final points, Jack invites members of the audience to partake of a free, no-obligation consultation at his office if they wish further guidance. They are contacted only if they fill out an evaluation form. "If you aren't interested, we aren't going to call you," he promises.

> *High level success requires getting yourself noticed.*

Johnson has become known in his community as the "senior citizen's licensed retirement counseling specialist." He works with nobody outside his specialty, but even that is not his primary differentiation. His differentiation and attraction as a service provider are a composite of many elements.

One of those elements is the timing of his one-hour post-seminar interviews. They start fifteen minutes after the hour or fifteen minutes before the hour – but never on the hour or the half-hour. Jack believes odd hours encourage people to arrive on time. He refuses to see clients who arrive more than ten minutes late. No exceptions are allowed. His receptionist meets late arrivers and informs them that they must reschedule. The next time, he notes, they are never late.

It might seem harsh, but Jack goes to some pains to make visitors feel special. They find a reserved parking space – with their name prominently displayed on it (along with the appointment time) – at the front entrance. A second person-alized welcome sign greets them in the lobby. A receptionist greets them by name, as does everyone they meet in the office. There is no mistake – they are honored guests.

He sends a handwritten note to every person who comes to his office for a consultation. He walks them to their cars. He sends flowers to the client after making a sale. He personally calls all three thousand clients on their birthdays – even when he's away from the office! When other professionals wonder where he finds the time, Jack replies simply, "I don't have time not to call them." He believes that the smallest differences are all about building his reputation: who he is, his uniqueness as a differentiated service provider. And he is right!

> *The smallest differences are all about building your reputation.*

Johnson believes that attention to the smallest differences defines your reputation. In so doing, he has become a local market brand of choice. Every year since 1990 he has received the insurance sales industry's highest recognition, the Million Dollar Round Table's "Top of the Table." (The honor requires at least three hundred fifty thousand dollars in earned commissions.) Johnson's two sons recently joined the business and are already qualifiers for "Top of the Table," a feat unmatched in an industry of more than ninety thousand providers. Jack no longer worries about burnout. After redefining his market and relaunching his reputation, he's having fun again.

Think about what types of experiences capture your attention. People never focus their attention to something similar to what they are accustomed. They notice what looks unique and different. The lesson is that you can't attempt to replicate what everyone else is doing in your business if you expect to gain a competitive advantage. Playing a "Me-Too" game is a losing proposition. Build a differentiation around something. Make it extraordinarily delightful and then communicate it to the same audience over and over. You can't over-communicate your difference. Just ask the professional, Jack Johnson. He knows. And so do his clients.

> *You can't over-communicate your difference.*

Filiep Sackx

I am often asked (actually, *challenged* might be the better word) whether I believe that the single greatest element for the success of a small business is found in the personality of the owner. The answer is an unequivocal "no."

Personality certainly adds a specific distinction to any business, no different from how different personalities may cause us to like or dislike an individual. But business success has far more to do with good strategy and systemization than personality, assuming of course that the number-one focus of the people running the business is on delighting *Systemization is critical for today's business success.*

the customer. Based on that assumption, a good strategy can be duplicated with the anticipation of achieving equally good results.

Filiep Sackx is a great example of duplicating a strategy with great success. A native of Belgium, Filiep was twenty-nine when he came to the United States in 1994. He found a job in the import/export business in San Jose, California, but after two years he wanted more. More income and more control of his time.

In 1997, recruited by a friend at a major financial services company, he began training for a career in the insurance and investment field. He worked hard and made a great start, earning more than fifty thousand dollars the first year and becoming recognized as one of the company's top local producers. But something still bothered Filiep. He wanted a higher level of success and he felt that somehow he needed to differentiate himself. He believed that "if you could draw the people to you, you didn't have to be a great closer. If you could attract them with a memorable experience, they would want to buy." Filiep's hunch was right. His income increased forty percent in 1998, and most of the increase came after October when he narrowed his focus to the senior market.

**Maintain
your focus.**

Beginning in 1999, Filiep vowed to maintain that focus, never working with anyone under the age of fifty-five. He made no exceptions, even when a client sought to refer his fifty-four-year-old brother to him. Filiep asked him to come back after his next birthday. The financial consultant firmly believed that compromising his focus even slightly would erode his reputation as "the specialist" within his market. He had learned a principle early in his career that most business owners never learn: Maintain your focus. He was right.

Like Jack Johnson, Filiep initiated regular educational events for prospective customers. He planned late-morning seminars twice a month, and he made them memorable. They took place in an elegant restaurant, never a hotel. Participants sat at a round table and were treated to a very nice lunch. There were door prizes, and of course everything was free. Many attendees asked to come back and bring a friend.

Before starting his entry into this market, Filiep assembled about six thousand names of prospects who fit a certain profile. They were all between the ages of fifty-nine and seventy-five; they were homeowners; and they had incomes of over fifty thousand dollars. He then began to brand his reputation into their minds. Every month, he sent invitations to those same six thousand people and every month he attracted thirty new attendees to his luncheon event. He altered the master prospect list only to add new names in the same number as had become clients.

Filiep also began collecting e-mail addresses of attendees, as well as those of all senior persons he met during the week. Then he started e-mailing his monthly seminar invitation to clients and past attendees, encouraging them to return, bring a friend or forward the e-mail message to a friend who might be interested. This simple little idea brought five or six additional people to the seminars each month.

> *He began collecting e-mail addresses from all of his attendees.*

Filiep sends a free monthly financial newsletter to all his clients and also to his six hundred highest-level prospects. That's the extent of his promotion, except for teaser ads in a local publication for seniors. The ads, which cost three hundred and fifty dollars a month, are not an advertisement for the seminar. Rather, they carry an emotional message about financial mistakes seniors make and they include a toll-free number to call to receive a free informational booklet. These little ads result in twelve to fifteen responses each month, and follow-up calls bring another five or six attendees to the seminars. Of course, this technique also fattens the mailing list.

There are three universal lessons that can be derived from Filiep's strategy:

1. To generate high-level success in today's market, you must differentiate yourself from the competition. (This is also called Market Separation.)
2. To implement a familiarization strategy, you must know the names of specific customers you want to attract.
3. To sustain success, you must systematize the way you operate.

Systemization guarantees predictability. And predictability is virtually absent from every human experience. Yet it is still a

> *Systemization guarantees predictability.*

non-negotiable component for building brand preference, a component that creates continued attraction and assures customers that they aren't making bad choices. It conveys a message that you know what you are doing.

Filiep Sacks doubled his income in 1999 and again in 2000. You've got to love those tangible results!

Kobey Corporation

Ivan M. Kobey began his career in the stock brokerage industry in the 1970s, transitioning to his current profession as a tax-planning strategist in 1991. Looking for ways to differentiate himself that year, he hit on the idea of publishing a daily half-page economic update that commented on stocks and interest rates.

KOBEY'S FINANCIAL UPDATE
05\03\00 11:00 AM EST

FINANCIAL NEWS SUMMARY: It's your economy - And - Investors are being confused by the choices - Where to put funds sitting on the side lines - The two year Treasury Note yielding 6.72% - Try to find a CD that is state tax free and yielding almost 6 and 3/4% - 30 year t/bonds yielding 6 04% while the ten year yields 6 32% - That's a 7 week high for the 10 year - Treasuries were hurt by the home sales number published Tuesday - Home sales at the fastest pace in 1 1/2 years - Home sales being driven by expectations the Fed will raise rates, not when, but, by how much - 1/4% or 1/2% - Place your bets - This writer sees another rate increase coming down the path soon after May's increase - Factory orders reported an increase of 2.2% - Analysts polled by Bloomberg News expected an increase - But, only 1.7% - This economy continues to fool many analysts - Does it not make sense that fear of higher prices drives consumers to action - Does to this writer - Does to those who hear me speak - Education is now an export - Foreign students pay to be educated - Buying services - Watch!

NYSE Dow Jones.......- 162.26 pts 10,569			30 yr Fixed Mortgage...................... 7 3/4 + 1			
NASDAQ................ - 125.33 pts 3,660			15 yr Fixed Mortgage...................... 7 1/2 + 1			
30 Year US Treasury.....................6.04%			1 year ARM .... 6 3/4 + 1			
Money Market Funds-Banks 3.50%			(Subject to **Market fluctuation** - Origination Fee not included)			
as quoted by: **NORWEST BANK**			quoted by: **Creative Mortgage Solutions, P.C.**			
6 month CD\365 day CD 3.40%			Trends qu-oted by Compak Trading as heard on KFNN Radio			
			Compak Trading 1-800-388-9700			
Tax deferred Annuity..................... 5, 6, 7%			Stocks - Employers in Arizona			
GOLD:............. UP@ $ 278.30	Intel .... - 3	11/16 Motorola............... - 2		American Express .+	11/16
SILVER: .... UP@ $ 5.08	Honeywell ....+	3/16 US West............... -		13/16 Safeway...............-	11/16
PLATINUM: .... DN@ $ 473.00	Banc One............-	11/16 Home Depot......... - 2		15/16 Microsoft............. -	15/16
KOBEY CORP A Problem Solving Firm			Sponsored and Paid by: Call: Michael Del Re			
E-mail: ikobey@kobey.com Web: www.xroadsmall.com/kobey/			**Creative Mortgage Solutions, P.C.** MB 0902090			
480-423-1096 800-280-1096			Call for info: (602) 728-0324/ Fax (602) 728-0399			
			1645 East Missouri , Suite 220 Phoenix, AZ. 85016			

A few local restaurants let Kobey put the first two hundred copies of his daily report on their tables during the lunch hour, and it wasn't long before the news media started referencing him as an economic futurist as well as an economic tax-planning strategist. Ivan's initiative neatly created a perception of his being an expert. (It doesn't hurt, either, that *The Arizona Republic* recently characterized Kobey's publication as part of the attractive ambience at the upscale Scottsdale restaurant Molly's-on-Main.)

These days, Ivan gives eight to ten speeches a week and his daily commentary has become so popular that he sends it out electronically to people around the country as well as placing it in area restaurants. Some Southwest financial firms have even started e-mailing it to their own client bases, an arrangement that benefits their reputations as well as Kobey's.

> *Differentiation builds perception and creates customer preference.*

Ivan's fee-for-service business focuses on tax planning strategies, and it has flourished. His daily half-page economic update has answered the question "Why Ivan?" in an occupational field that has numerous competitors. Even more significantly, he answered that question for most clients even before meeting them. Ivan is a superb example of our tag line, "Getting the Consumer to Notice You First!"

William V. Thompson & Associates

When William Thompson dreamed of opening his own accounting office, he found just the inspiration he needed at church.

The year was 1990 and William was nine years into his career, first at Ernst & Young and then with the leading hosiery producer Kayser-Roth in Greensboro, North Carolina. He also was very involved in his church, the Evangel Fellowship, where he became acutely aware of the average church's need for expert guidance on tax law and accounting. He knew of no specialists in this area. The need was apparent, at least to him, and it wasn't long before his heart, with the support of his wife, would encourage him to take the plunge.

William left Kayser-Roth in 1990 and opened a modest office. His church was his first client, and referrals from his pastor, Dr. Otis Locket Sr., initially sustained his growth. He knew, however, that the kind of success he wanted would require more than a few calls to local ministers. Somehow, he needed to stand out from the crowd of CPAs and accountants who already cluttered the landscape. He felt he needed to create a distinct presence in order to visibly position himself above the competition.

> *You have to stand out from the crowd of competitors.*

It took very little investigation to find out that the General Baptist denomination had more than two thousand member churches, divided into some two hundred associations. Thompson began sending letters to them, offering to give free presentations at their quarterly church conferences. The result was thirty to fifty engagements a year, a demand that continues to this day. William accepted every request. Some were hours away. Some were limited to fifteen-minute presentations, others an hour. They all added up to building a reputation that eventually preceded him. His business began to flourish and his heart's zeal for providing value to his faith was being fulfilled.

By 1995, Thompson had a clientele of four hundred churches. Individual pastors were inquiring into the possibility of his teaching general financial planning and tax-assistance classes to their congregations, as well as helping them on a personal basis. Just a few months later, William began his first two-hour Friday night class, which quickly evolved into a Friday night/Saturday morning program.

At this point he was fairly well known. But he knew that this was no time – nor would it ever be, actually – to rely on his reputation alone to grow his practice. Unlike so many professionals and business owners, he realized he must keep connecting and intensifying relationships with clients and prospects. He regularly met with clients twice a year, but he could see now that he needed to stay in touch more frequently. William concluded that though most of them had been initially attracted to him through his presentations, increasing their loyalty and maintaining his market dominance would require no less.

> *Continually connecting will always intensify your relationship.*

William began maintaining contact with clients and non-clients by including all of them on his mailing list that announced his free quarterly community workshops. Whether they came or not was not the issue. It was as important to him to maintain consistent and frequent communication – which also reminded them of his professional reputation – as to fill seats. But he did fill seats. His workshops typically attracted some eighty people.

In 1995, Thompson decided to move into publishing pamphlets. His first, "The Word on Money," counseled individuals on how to cut expenses and control, manage and create money. His second pamphlet, "The Ninety-Nine Most Common Violations Committed by the Church and Clergy," identified the most common financial errors churches make. Both publications were highly successful and highly recognized within the denomination, further securing his reputation as a specialist, especially for people within the church family.

Since then, William has branched out into self-published books, audio recordings and e-mail. He is the author of three books: *The Church, the Clergy & the IRS* (1998); *Principles, Promises & Power – Possessing Your Inheritance* (1998); and *Debt Trap – How Did We Get In? How Do We Get Out?* (1999). He

> *Clients never complain about too much contact.*

has also recorded a three-cassette program called *"Trading 4 Profit$"* to accompany his recently extended ten-week workshop of the same name. Maybe more important, this energetic entrepreneur has begun sending biweekly e-mail news broadcasts – something any business owner could easily do. William knows that clients never complain about too much contact. Absence doesn't make the heart grow fonder – but it will make a client grow distant and eventually bitter.

The basic elements of Identity Branding never change for anyone, regardless of profession or business.
1. Identify a name-specific audience
2. Create an experience that visibly accentuates your differentiation and attracts the prospect to you
3. Employ a strategy to continually connect with your

name-specific audience, with frequency and consistency, in order to establish mindshare as the brand of choice

> *Identity Branding always has a beginning, but never an ending.*

From his humble beginning only ten years ago, William has grown his accounting firm to seven employees. His strategy was to differentiate himself, get publicly noticed and then intensify the relationships as he progressed. The strategy of *Identity Branding* always has a beginning but – as William found out – it never has an ending. It just gets revised and re-created. And if you have a name-specific audience to target, you'll find they get friendlier, easier to access and more loyal. It's a great combination that creates a rewarding relationship for all. By focusing on giving instead of getting, William has not only thrived in business but also has made a positive impact on all the lives he touches. A job well done!

A Nice Touch ... or Much More?

The customer doesn't always consciously recognize those things businesses use to create visible differentiation. Sometimes it seems too simple – a "nice touch" rather than a serious, well-planned strategy. But the impact is powerful. As these examples illustrate, distinction identifiers build intrigue, customer loyalty and brand preference.

> *"Simple" extra touches can carry a powerful impact.*

DOUBLETREE HOTELS created incredible customer loyalty and likability by giving every guest a package of chocolate chip cookies at check-in. This "nice touch" has become the chain's trademark. Sounds like a small differentiator but the impact is huge, as I can tell you from talking to fellow business travelers. They really look forward to those cookies at the end of a hectic day – enough that it influences their booking decisions. What do you do to build likability?

COURTYARD BY MARRIOTT has numerous strategies for creating a distinction, but for some Marriotts, one little extra starts with requesting your business card at check-in. At check-out, you receive the card back – now laminated and turned into a luggage tag (with hotel information and thank-you message on the reverse). The investment is incredibly cheap (about fifty dollars for a lamination machine and a dime's worth of material per tag). It's also fast, taking less than a minute to assemble each tag.

EMBASSY SUITES pioneered the all-suite concept and then took it a step further – offering guests a free morning breakfast and a free evening cocktail hour. It was one of the first visible distinctions a hotel ever implemented. Yes, others have followed their example, but first is always better than better. They still are and will remain the noted "king" of this strategy. Everyone else is an imitation. What are you doing that is visibly different from your competition?

> *Collect your customer's e-mail addresses.*

LEGAL SEA FOODS instantly drew rave reviews with the opening of its first restaurant in 1968, and the accolades have continued apace ever since. The Boston-based restaurant chain's chowder was served at the presidential inauguration in 1981. In 1986, NBC's "Today" show called it the best seafood restaurant in America. You would think that this name recognition would be sufficient to attract business, but in 2001 the restaurant

We respect your privacy. We won't give (or sell) your name, address, or any other data to any other organization no matter how much they beg us or plead. No, not even if they offer us obscene amounts of money. It's strictly between us. We hope you enjoy the recipes and special events.

"*If it isn't fresh, it isn't Legal!*"

implemented a new strategy aimed at deepening customer loyalty. It's really simple. Waiters just ask diners for their e-mail addresses. Then, every two weeks, these customers receive an e-mail message from Legal Sea Foods. The e-mail features a copy of the monthly special menu, various newsworthy information, a recipe and possibly a coupon. The restaurant understands that business success is related to marketing and that there are simply too many choices to take customer loyalty for granted. Most business owners don't seem to know this. They think that a satisfied customer is enough to win future business. Not Legal Sea Foods. They want to maximize their appeal and their future business by constantly increasing mindshare even with those who know them well. How do you connect with your customers?

FARM BUREAU FINANCIAL SERVICES gained recognition in American Falls, Idaho, when a number of agents in the Monte Watson Insurance Agency figured out how to differentiate themselves in an industry that's all too often associated with blandness. With Halloween approaching, the agents secured a tractor-trailer truckload of pumpkins and announced a pumpkin giveaway for the children of American Falls. Almost instantly, this goodwill gesture evolved into an annual citywide affair. The local newspaper was so impressed, it practically portrayed the event as a public service. The excitement spawned a pumpkin-painting contest that was so large it was featured prominently in the newspaper with numerous pictures and articles.

Farm Bureau's objective – to build prospect affection by giving back to the community instead of just focusing on getting – paid off in a big way. Giving free pumpkins to children, while at the same time capturing the names of the kids' parents, was an easy way to initiate a long-term courting strategy. These ingenious marketers suddenly had a large new roster of targeted prospects to send

> *When you are "first" you can position everyone else as an imitation.*

periodical information about financial subjects such as college savings programs and wealth strategy plans. Do you think these Farm Bureau agents enhanced their chances of securing future appointments? Do you think they're building a competitive advantage – a perception of genuine caring and likability? Imagine next year sending an e-mail to announce the annual pumpkin giveaway again. Farm Bureau knows that consistent visibility is what creates credibility.

The way the agents followed through on their brilliant promotion illustrates the absolutely crucial importance of not squandering opportunities. They had a mechanism in place for capturing names and a strategy for courting the audience that was initially impacted. After all, how much bigger impact can you make than when the children of American Falls, who previously thought that pumpkins grew in pumpkin patches, now know differently! They know that, in their community, pumpkins come from the Farm Bureau Insurance agents.

Here's a bonus idea to boost these parents' recognition and appreciation of you. Take a bunch of candid digital photographs while the children are having fun picking out their pumpkins, then load the photos into a e-mail photo album at www.my-ecustomer.com. The Web site provides an e-mail photo album that you can name. Send the web link to the parents, thanking them for sharing their children with you and for participating in the "Almost Famous Pumpkin Giveaway." This is called a tag line. Parents can download the pictures. It's another way to create deeper appreciation and to accentuate you as different from the competition. Just think of all the events where you could use this technique. Church picnic, golf tournaments, sports events, etc.

ENTERPRISE RENT-A-CAR is much more than a business that provides cars for individuals needing transportation. Not just concerned with getting a sale, this company knows it is much more important to get the customer to want to do business with them, not only now but in the future. To accomplish this, Enterprise focuses instead on building a distinctive impression – an exceptional attraction – on the people whose lives it touches.

> *Focus on getting the customer to want to do business with you, not just on getting a transaction.*

Here are a couple of examples. On St. Valentine's Day, Judson Nix, assistant manager of Enterprise's Mobile, Alabama, office, took carnations to all of the employees in corporate offices that sent customers to him over the year. Twice in one month, Enterprise manager Ryan Krumroy in Kernersville, North Carolina, delivered donuts and pizza to auto repair shops, insurance claim offices and corporate clients with whom he wanted to build deeper loyalty and preference.

What's going on here? Once-in-awhile acts of kindness casually hatched by two of Enterprise's top managers? Hardly. The ideas actually grew out of the company's manager training program – a weekly directive to strategize how to impact the lives of people who make them successful. Along with weekly sales results, every Enterprise office regularly reports what it has done to create affection with existing customers and "want-to-have-as-customer" prospects.

> *Focus on adding value to your customers' lives.*

Managers are taught how to add value to their customers' lives in personal ways as well as through good business practices. That's called "giving," and it begins the branding process, building deep mindshare with activities that delight and surprise the recipients.

Enterprise Rent-a-Car knows that providing quality cars and quality service is not enough. It believes you must position yourself as different, distinct and more caring than the competition. Has it paid off? Ten years ago, you might not even have heard of Enterprise. Five years ago, you probably never saw Enterprise at an airport. Today, Enterprise is the largest car rental company in North America. A well-kept secret? Not to the people who get donuts, pizzas and carnations on a regular basis. It's their favorite car rental company, the one that cares more than just about making another transaction.

THE FRESH MARKET is a chain of boutique grocery stores in the Southeast known for coziness (just twenty thousand square feet of floor space), premium specialty foods and high-toned ambience. The lighting is subtle, the musical background classical. Customers are invited to sip gourmet coffee as they shop. Not only is the coffee freshly brewed (every ten minutes) but the coffee table is immaculate and lavishly stocked with sweeteners and real cream (in a pewter pitcher).

> *The customer, not your product display, is your primary focus.*

Floor space is consciously sacrificed to increase customer appeal. Aisles are arranged diagonally and are noticeably wider than the usual supermarket setup. To many retailers, this is an academic no-no, since all retailers know that this foolish oversight sacrifices about twenty percent of what could be product display space – certainly not the wise thing to do if you want to sell more product, right? But the Fresh Market bets on being able to create more sales by designing a store that creates a luring appeal to the customer to return. Imagine that – placing the customer ahead of the product!

Most grocery stories only place employees behind counters, and the counters are built directly horizontal to wall space. At the Fresh Market, the counters curve and they're much smaller and intimate than most stores. Also, they're located not only along walls but also in the center of the store. These oasis counters are staffed with employees ready to assist with coffee beans, bulk candy, spices or such.

The "end of the shopping experience" will define the entire shopping conclusion.

The checkout experience is just as impressive. When there are more than two people in line, another cashier point is opened. Whichever employee is closest to the checkout line usually jumps in without being asked. Very rarely does anyone need to signal for help. These employees have been taught that the "end of the shopping experience," the final event, will define the entire shopping conclusion. A customer either leaves with fond memories of a great experience or they leave irritated by being forced to wait – with all feelings of good will erased.

The thirty-store (and growing) grocery chain's performance has been remarkable. In 2001 it reported nine percent annual growth and one hundred and ninety-three million dollars in sales. Those results are enviable compared to most grocery stores, especially when you consider that customers return knowing that they are paying a premium price.

Whoever said that the customer is far more concerned with the experience they are purchasing than the product attached to it? What's the experience you're providing? Is it distinct or just another "Me-Too ... oh, yeah ... But-Better."

Summary Reflections

You must do something that is distinctively different and almost outrageously visible to gain attention in today's excessive and irritating advertising barrage in America.

Today's success-strategy requires focusing on the process of building an "experience of powerful attraction" visibly apparent to the customer.

A satisfied customer is no longer enough to assure that they will return.

Differentiation is not an option for success.

You can't over communicate your difference.

Even unique product features and benefits no longer give you "the edge."

Traditional advertising is less effective today than any time in history.

Focusing on increasing your company's operational efficiency may be necessary, but it will not attract new customers.

Every business has a strategic alliance opportunity(s) with another business. What's yours?

The frequency of your customer connection determines the

degree of preference your customer will develop for you.

Narrowing your market focus (product and service) will broaden your appeal to the public.

Business success is far more dependent on marketing strategy than on personality or on your offering, assuming it is of acceptable quality.

Systemizing your marketing strategy guarantees predictability and attraction.

A branding strategy always has a beginning, but never an ending.

If you're "first" in your offering, announce it, accentuate it, tag-line it and keep announcing it. Let it become part of your core message. First is always better than better. It is even better than BEST. Claiming "first," positions everyone else as an imitation.

The following business categories were reviewed in this chapter. What ideas could you adapt to your business?

- Car Repair
- Restaurant
- Gourmet Food Store
- Construction Company
- Oil Distribution Company
- Manufacturing Company
- Retirement Planning Professional
- Investment Specialist
- Tax Strategist
- Accountant
- Boutique Grocery Store

Brilliant Strategies Notebook

My thoughts on how to apply this chapter's lessons to my business...

"Without a customer and potential customer name-specific database, it is practically impossible to begin a courting process for building preference for you, much less be able to measure the effectiveness of your marketing strategy."

Robert F. Krumroy

Chapter Eight

Building a Name-Specific Database

Great marketers know that marketing is not about their company's product. It's about the company's customer or the potential customer they are trying to attract. It's about building a relationship with customers and potential customers, and not just when you encounter them face-to-face but on an ongoing basis. Some say that marketing is like a foot race. The last step may determine the winner, but the effectiveness of all of your strides determines the chances of your success, way before you reach the finish line. Others say that great marketing is like a great marriage. The depth of the relationship is hardy identifiable by its individual components, but the individuals who make it happen are always conscious of their efforts to please the other person, to show they care.

> *Marketing is not about your product. It's about your customer.*

Great marketers connect with their customers frequently with the goal of delighting them and creating intensified relationships. After all, most people today are hesitant to transact business with strangers. The barrage of intrusion marketing has made everyone a skeptic. To maximize your results, people need to hear about you before they encounter you for the first time, and then continuously after that. Your objective must be to enter their world of familiarity, and the more frequently they hear about you the more success you can expect.

> *Great marketers connect with their customers frequently.*

One of the critical truths in business today is this: Your degree of attractability is going to be in direct proportion to your degree of visibility, and visibility is the single most important element in creating credibility. Great marketers become recognizable over time because of their visibility. Until you become visible, you will not be credible and neither will you be attractive in the customer's mind. Since visibility creates attraction, if you are waiting for customers to somehow notice you on their own in this overcrowded marketplace, you are going to pay a horrible price.

> *Consistent visibility creates attraction.*

Remember, great marketing for the small-business owner is not dependent on creating visibility through advertising. (Look at Starbucks. It has never run an advertisement. The company depends on a narrow focus and a differentiated reputation for creating customer attraction.) Neither is great marketing about providing the customer with another look-alike brochure, business card, direct-mail letter or newspaper insert coupon. And it is no longer enough for business owners to identify their desired market as a general demographic category and then attempt to somehow expose this demographic category to their business through traditional, non-personal media exposure. Today, success requires more.

Most businesses can no longer afford to wait until they encounter "buying customers" as their beginning point for securing names for their database. If you want to experience high-level success in your business, it is important to find and accumulate specific names of potential customers before you meet them or before they have walked through the doors of your business. Finding and accumulating names,

> *Find and accumulate specific names of potential customers.*

both those of customers and potential customers, must become the initial and primary component to building your business preference through a planned attraction strategy.

It is not difficult to begin accumulating names of your actual customers, though it will require an execution of strategy. A restaurant owner, or any business owner, may decide to simply print a three-by-five promotional card that a customer fills out in exchange for a perforated coupon they can use for their next visit. Another business may simply request a name and address registration at the time of purchase in exchange for monthly information mailings or mailed announcements of special events, sales or promotions. Whatever means you select, don't forget to get e-mail addresses. It takes no extra effort and may prove to be your most cost-effective method to broadcast special events, news, coupons, thank-you messages, birthday wishes, etc.

Don't forget the most obvious and easiest places to get potential customer names. Nearly every organization has a member directory that includes e-mail addresses. Just for starters, you've got the chamber of commerce (most membership directories are now on the internet), civic clubs, occupational associations, merchants association, arts council, United Way contributors, even your place of worship. You can easily use these names as long as you're

> *Your job is to begin a courting process.*

not going to obnoxiously "ambush" them. Just remember that your job is to begin a courting process with the potential customer that creates a compelling association, not a repelling association. Make your contacts delightful and intriguing, and no one will complain.

Your initial giving approach will get far more than the competition's typical get approach.

Another idea, used occasionally but not frequently enough by salespeople, is to call on a newly established business with a gift of doughnuts in hand. (You can get information about new businesses from newspaper announcements or the chamber of commerce.) Imagine doing this every week as a means to introduce yourself with a gesture of giving-versus-getting. Now, begin your strategy of consistent connection to build preference over time. But be ready, many business owners will express interest in what you do when you initially deliver the doughnuts. Trust me, your initial giving approach will get far more than the competition's typical get approach.

Here's another possibility to consider. Very few organizations that hold recurring events such as silent auctions, holiday dances or fish fries ever develop a database of attendees. The consequence is that next year's new chairperson has to start from scratch trying to attract people to the function. Offer to register people and put their information into an official database for the organization so that they have a starting point for next year's function. You will be a hero, plus you are well on your way to finding name-specific prospects for your business.

Here are a few more creative approaches businesses have used to build databases, and all have proven successful.

E-mail Capture for Existing Customers

This scenario concerns a property and casualty insurance agency with more than forty-two hundred customers. However, the application is universal to any business that has customers and wants a creative way to obtain their e-mail addresses.

Don was one of his company's most successful insurance agents. He established uniqueness in the market by writing his own newsletter every month and holding investment seminars and fusion marketing events for clients four to six times a year. He understood the importance of maintaining frequent contact with his large customer base and encouraging referrals, but the newsletters and invitations were taking up a lot of time and money. Printing, folding, stamping and inserting were time intensive and expensive. It was time to start using e-mail as the primary connection tool, and we showed him how.

Don got the process underway by offering one of his administrative assistants a challenge. He would pay her fifty cents for each e-mail address if she could complete at least eighty percent of the client list within a month. He gave her free rein to make the calls anytime she wished – day, night or weekends, working the assignment around her regular duties. At the end of four weeks, Debbie had collected three thousand seven hundred e-mail addresses and earned a bonus of eighteen hundred fifty dollars. For Don the work was invaluable. Less than a year later, he is e-mailing information and invitations to more than six thousand people, including fifteen hundred prospects, each month.

> *3,700 e-mail addresses were collected in four weeks. The majority of your customers have one.*

Those without access to administrative staff could hire high school students. One business owner paid his teenage daughter's Sunday school class to do the job as a money-raising project for their summer beach weekend. Not only did he get the job done, accumulating more than twenty-two hundred e-mail addresses, but he also supported a cause that was close to his heart.

Non-Golfing Golf Tournament (New Name Capture)

For many businesses, capturing the names of people who will eventually need your product or service is well worth the effort. You can then include them in your strategy to pre-establish market preference. An inexpensive name identification and promotion strategy is to participate in sponsoring a local golf tournament.

Don't golf in a golf tournament!

Most country clubs, semi-private courses and public links are in the market for sponsors, and the fees are usually nominal. Just call any course to find out what groups are organizing tournaments and to get the names of contact people. You can choose those that make sense for your business.

An example might be the yearly tourney put on by the Enterprise Rent-a-Car office in appreciation of the owners of car repair shops, auto parts companies, insurance agencies, financing companies and others that consistently send business to them. With their above-average incomes (business owners and their key employees), these people make great prospective customers for most businesses. Having their names, addresses and e-mail will allow you to influence them with a marketing strategy.

The first rule, however, is to stay out of the play. Instead of signing up for a foursome, sponsor one of the "watering holes" that cater to golfers as they pass by. These sponsorships typically cost only one hundred to two hundred dollars. The organization supplies the ice-cold beer and soft drinks. You just need to get a lawn chair, wait to greet the foursomes as they make the rounds and hand out the beverages. Also bring along a quantity of cigars, the one-dollar golf specials. Any cigar shop can help you out – many will even donate the cigars or show up at the event and co-sponsor it with you. (To not leave anyone out, offer bubblegum cigars as well as the tobacco version.)

If the cigars don't appeal to you, ask to sponsor the tournament's hole-in-one car give-away. This is an especially great idea if you've got a sense of humor. When a foursome approaches, you guarantee that one of them will win the car that's sitting there. It's a story you will tell to all of the foursomes that come by. You vow that even if nobody scores a hole-in-one, the car will be awarded to whoever comes closest.

Now, the key is finding out in advance what kind of car will be displayed. Then go to a toy store and purchase matchbox car replicates. Have one in your pocket for your presentation after the last of the golfers take their best shots.

> *Send a free e-mail photo album to the participants.*

Have a camera handy and take a picture of every foursome. If you do the matchbox car idea, have the "winner" pose on bended knee in front of the other three golfers, proudly displaying his new car. It's pure silliness and they will love it. You are already starting to delight the customer. Then collect their mail and e-mail information so you can send them prints of the photos and an e-mail link where a free photo album of the entire tournament will be posted (www.my-ecustomer.com). When you send along the photos, include a letter that thanks them for taking part in the fund-raiser and also announces both the golfing and financial results of the event. You may want to hand-deliver some of these letters, particularly to the golfers who asked questions about you and your business.

> ### *Delight customers away from the competition.*

One of our clients took part in nine tournaments over a four-month period and used this approach to gather more than sixteen hundred names of highly paid professionals. He tracked the business profits from this group of people and in six months had acquired some thirty thousand dollars of profits from the additional sales. A year later, using ideas like this to capture names, he had amassed more than three thousand names in his database. It's his belief now that he's not *selling* anymore, but rather *delighting* customers away from the competition!

Child Identification Day

Holding a "Child Identification Day" is another very effective way to accumulate names for your database, while at the same time creating feelings of affection by those you impact. This program has been conducted at private schools, daycare centers, city-sponsored recreational sport teams, churches, synagogues, and even at actual places of business – if your business has high traffic.

The Web site, www.childsid.com (owned by Polaroid), provides a step-by-step instructional guide on "How to Host a KidCare ID Event," and it's complete with news releases, newspaper ads, letters and signs for promoting your event. The average cost of the kits is about a buck-fifty per child – which can be paid by you or by the parent – and the kits can be customized with your name on them if ordered in quantities of three hundred. The local police department will even fingerprint the children by providing "explorers" (high school seniors who are going to the police academy) to help.

It's easy to get a child ID kit and a brochure to show the program to the organization you want to conduct this with. Once approved, parents fill out an authorization form with address, phone and e-mail address. Include on the form a statement that reads, "Unless I check the box below, you have my authorization to e-mail me occasional information on special offers and information which you believe may be of interest."

Now that you have built a name-specific database, established your presence, giving value by providing their child with an identi-fication tag – including picture and finger-printing – it is pretty simple to initiate a future communication strategy. After all, you

> *Initiate a future communication strategy.*

gave them value without expecting anything in return. That never goes unnoticed. It is the beginning of building preference and likability over the competition.

Summary Reflections

Every person is not a potentially equally profitable customer. Marketing is about building a meaningful relationship to a targeted audience. It is not about trying to get noticed by everyone in your city.

Credibility and attractibility are in direct proportion to your visibility.

Without a targeted, name-specific client and prospect database, it is impossible to initiate a meaningful courting strategy.

Find a way to obtain your customer and targeted prospect e-mail addresses.

Where can you find potential customer names and addresses?

- Chamber of Commerce members
- Merchant Associations
- Occupational Associations
- Civic and Social Clubs
- Affinity Groups
- Religious Organizations

What activities can you participate in, or conduct, to attract future customers and capture their contact information?

Purchase a digital camera, take candid pictures at an event

and e-mail your potential customers an e-mail photo album as a way of creating uniqueness and appreciation.

Stop selling! Start delighting the customer away from the competition. Focus on getting the customer to want to buy.

Brilliant Strategies Notebook

My thoughts on how to apply this chapter's lessons to my business...

_____

_____

_____

_____

_____

_____

_____

_____

_____

_____

_____

_____

_____

_____

_____

_____

_____

_____

_____

_____

_____

_____

_____

_____

"Don't get duped into believing that print advertising, the conventional solution to market visibility, will create market dominance. It only reinforces it once attained.

For most small businesses and professionals, print advertising should be the last component of your marketing strategy, if at all – not the first."

Robert F. Krumroy

Fusion Marketing Strategies

Wouldn't you like to make somebody else's customers yours? That's the whole idea behind fusion marketing, or what some refer to as alliance marketing, and it's long been a strategy for many businesses.

Years ago, when Pepsi purchased Taco Bell, it was a strategy to capture a larger percentage of the beverage market in the fast-food segment of America. This particular "merger" may have been a bad business decision, increasing their product breadth outside of their expertise and blurring their company's core business. But there are great examples of other companies that have concluded that a business expansion through a merger or acquisition isn't necessary to increase customer appeal, increase sales or increase customer satisfaction. A simple marketing business alliance with the right "partner" will more than suffice.

Make somebody else's customer yours!

You only have to look at Starbucks and Barnes & Noble to see how successful this kind of partnering can be. Someone had the foresight to recognize that people who were willing to pay three dollars and fifty cents for a cup of coffee could also afford expensive books. And if Barnes & Noble had clients that could afford to buy expensive books, they could probably afford to buy expensive coffee. Plus, both companies didn't have all of the same customers. So, if an alliance could attract greater numbers of customers for each business; if they could get customers to spend longer time in any one place and see each company's products more often; they would probably buy more product, coffee and books – not to mention the "likability" increase the customer experiences. They were right.

Creating an alliance can increase customer preference and familiarity.

The longer customers stay in a store, the greater chance they will buy. Likewise, the more that customers personally interact with you (assuming they like the person, the place or the product) the greater chance they will establish a preference for you and your business. It's back to the courting analogy: Visibility establishes credibility. No preferential attraction is established if your customers rarely see you and you fail to create attention.

It is not about increasing your company's name recognition. It is about creating a visible differentiation compared to the competition. The greater the differentiation, the greater the positive effect on attraction.

Creating a Healthy Alliance

Greg Eason and Bobby Layne own and manage a health supplement store called Health Nuts. It's a business that caters to customers who care about their long-term health, and the proprietors have gained a reputation for taking extra time to answer questions and learning their products in depth (much more than the typical health store employee who more often than not reads the label to you when you ask a question). Still, they saw increasing competition and knew they had to do a better job of marketing themselves.

Enter Gary Bargebuhr, a certified financial planner who had climbed the ladder of success in record time. By 2000, ten years after joining Shearson Lehman Hutton, he had worked his way to the top twenty-five percent of investment brokerage representatives in the industry. Gary out-produced

> *Develop a highly recognizable personal business image.*

other brokers with far more years of experience, and he did it by focusing not on selling but on intentionally developing an intriguing personal business image, a local celebrity-type identity that caused the customer to want to buy.

A frequent customer of Health Nuts, Bargebuhr couldn't help making observations about the clientele he saw in the store. They were obviously successful, and more than that they weren't interested in some quick-fix formula for staying healthy. He saw a direct parallel between them and his financial clients, who also focused on long-term results as their primary component for investment advice. He couldn't help thinking that it would be good for everyone to expose these similarly minded customers to the other's business.

Like Gary, Healthnuts' Greg Eason and Bobby Layne were also interested in adding long-term value for their clients. They knew the importance of building relationships; they knew it took more than an occasional encounter at the cash register to sustain loyalty. They felt that if they could accentuate their genuine caring for the community, be visibly seen as adding value (with no agenda of trying to profit) and do something that was intriguingly different, whether or not the customer took advantage of the offering was not the issue. The big benefit was that everyone would recognize the gesture, the differentiation and the good will.

> A satisfactory purchasing experience doesn't sustain customer loyalty.

As part of their alliance, Gary Bargebuhr and Health Nuts merged their client lists into one database of more than one thousand names and used it to send out invitations to a financial planning seminar. They also placed a few hundred more flyers about the seminar at the store's cash register, easily accessible to customers and convenient for the checkout person to deposit in bags. The seminars have been a great success, bringing new business to both partners of the alliance and increasing the frequency of the customer connection. When that happens, you automatically attain a greater degree of mindshare, customer loyalty and increased sales.

This example is no different from a retail store's need to frequently change its display windows. When customers see "action" in a business, whether it directly involves them or not, their conclusion is: "This must be a dynamic business,

A Complementary Seminar For Our Valued Customers

Thursday Evening, October 4th, 6:30pm
Health Nuts Natural Foods and Juice Bar, Greensboro NC

Saturday Morning, October 6th, 10am
Starmount Forest Country Club, Greensboro NC

"Smart Women Finish Rich"
It's fun   It's simple   It's easy to learn and use.

Profile Today
*There are 34 million women above the age of 50 in the U.S. today.
*There is a 3:2 ratio of women to men above the age of 50.
*For women turning 65, the average remaining life expectancy is over 22 more years.
*9 out of 10 women will be forced to manage their own money due to divorce, being single, or widowhood.
*57.5 million women work, 42 million being full time

Widowhood
*The average age of widowhood is 56.
*A widow lives an average of 18 years after her husband's death.
*25% of widows go through the death benefits left by a husband within two months.
*82% of all 85+ year old women are widowed.

continued on back

The seminar was developed in conjunction with David L. Bach, the author of the best selling book "Smart Women Finish Rich".
Gary L. Bargebuhr, CFP is with Salomon Smith Barney in Greensboro, North Carolina. He has been an investment consultant for 15 years and enjoys teaching seminars. Gary is also a customer of Health Nuts who benefits from the products he purchases from us.
The presentation is both very informative and entertaining.
Literally thousands of women around the country have attended the seminar and are using the tools they learned to take charge of their financial future.

one that I am glad to be (or maybe need to be) connected to, one that I should pay attention to. After all, I wouldn't want to miss out on something."

It's no wonder that Gary has risen to the top ranks of the investment industry. He creates intrigue; he's special and his clients know it.

More Fusion Strategies

> *Great marketers embrace creativity.*

Business owners who are great marketers embrace creativity. They instinctively know that sameness creates no attraction and that what worked yesterday won't work tomorrow. This new breed of highly successful business owners enthusiastically seek out new ideas, many times implementing them while still in the evaluation stage. They understand that waiting to completely analyze an idea may reduce risk, but it will also reduce potential success – eliminating opportunities that can then be grabbed by their competition unless they act quickly.

Just as product advantages have a shelf life of about sixty days, so too do brilliant marketing strategies have a window of opportunity – opportunities that can disappear quickly. The old saying that "haste makes waste" is still applicable. Business ownership is not for the reckless, but in today's marketing environment, neither is it for the timid, the overly cautious or the person not wanting to enthusiastically experiment with new ideas – not in an overcrowded sea of competition.

> *Sameness creates no attraction.*

How "different" do you need to be? Be courageous. The more that people tell you an idea is crazy, the closer you are to hitting onto something that will produce an unbelievable marketing advantage. Over the years I have talked to hundreds of people who successfully created marketing alliances. Here are a few of them.

The Bookstore Alliance

A financial advisor who wanted to work exclusively with clients who shared his religious values found a willing partner in a Christian bookstore. You might say it was an alliance made in heaven. They believed in the same theology, supported the same organizations and more than likely shared some of the same clients. One of their first decisions was to sponsor a special appreciation event for bookstore customers that would delight both them and their children. They found a winner in "Child's Morning Out."

The initiative got underway with a mass mailing to bookstore customers and clients of the financial advisor. The thank-you letter announced plans for a free showing of a first-run movie on a forthcoming Saturday morning. The children of the customers and clients were eligible to attend, and each of them was also encouraged to bring a friend. The alliance partners contacted a movie theater and purchased an entire mid-morning showing of a new release, a biblically themed animated film. Since the theater normally didn't open until after noon, it charged only four hundred to five hundred dollars for the screening.

> *Branding always begins with an experience.*

The financial planner lined up members of his church's youth group to escort the children into the theater as their parents dropped them off at curbside. That cost: a two hundred dollar contribution to the group's summer beach trip fund. A local doughnut shop contributed a doughnut in a plastic bag for each child, stapling a dollar coupon to it. Before the movie started, there was a drawing for door prizes. The theatre donated ten free movie tickets. The bookstore chipped in five ten-dollar gift certificates.

Along with the initial mailer, additional flyers were handed out at the bookstore's cash register three weeks before the event. The flyers included a message about the alliance partners' commitment to values and their appreciation for customers.

The parents registered their children for the event by visiting the bookstore on a designated Saturday. The response was overwhelming. By 10 a.m. on registration morning, the showing was fully booked. By noon, the sponsors were on the phone to the theater to book three additional showings. It must have been a scene, with more than nine hundred parents registering their children and their children's friends while many other customers looked on at this grand gesture.

Customer registration forms create a database for future connection.

The registration forms (parent's name, address, phone number and e-mail address) created a database for future connection and served as the child's entry form for the prize drawings. "Child's Morning Out" now takes place three times per year. It is an identifying business image, uniquely identified with both the bookstore and the financial planner.

The goal of marketing is to appear unique, to attract new prospects and to create deeper loyalty from existing customers. Branding always begins with an experience that creates the perception that you and your product are incomparable.

The Choosing-a-College Alliance

Always ally yourself with someone who desires the same type of exposure to similar types of prospects. A yearly seminar on

"How to Help Your Child Choose a College" could be compatibly co-sponsored by a computer business, sporting goods store, youth-oriented clothing shop or financial planner, perhaps joined as well by a psychologist and college representatives. The cost would be minimal if held in a library, school or college. Letters, e-mails and flyers in the participating stores would invite parents of school-age students to attend. You could also contact local high schools, asking them to participate and also to promote the event to juniors and seniors.

The Annual Forecast Meeting

Another effective marketing idea is to become known (do it consistently!) for conducting an annual event at the beginning of each year. Such as "The Best Investments and Best All-Inclusive Vacations for the New Year." A local bank, mortgage broker, financial planner or stockbroker could assemble a mutual client mailing list, combining their names with those of a travel company. Announce that this is your "Almost Famous Annual Great Dessert Extravaganza" – an event not to be missed. Bring a friend! All would share the costs and also share in the exposure to a multitude of enthusiastic potential clients. Throw in a few door prizes – bottles of wine, a catered dinner, gift certificates – and watch clients return year after year. It's important to make it fun, to separate yourself from the sameness, the normal blandness of your competition or your industry. People don't come back to seminars or workshops (most don't even come the first time), but they do come back to "events."

> *Be creative!*
> *Let your mind*
> *run wild!*

The Wine Tasting Event

Wine merchants mix well with creative marketing ideas. How about "A Taste of Wine for the Autumn Times – An Evening of Wine Tasting and Investment Tips." Guess who provides the wine for free? The wine merchant! For a spring theme, consider a client appreciation event called "Croquet and Chardonnay – Wear Your English Whites for a Fun Evening of Merriment." Let them know that this is a "Friends Bringing Friends" event or a "Client Appreciation" night. And be sure to encourage them to bring guests.

I have seen alliances between art galleries and commercial photographers, coupled with a wine tasting, inviting business owners to an evening reception to view artwork and the newest techniques for advertising their products. I have seen landscape companies and home renovation companies share the spotlight in a customer event. I have seen wine merchants more than happy to conduct an extensive free wine tasting while paired up with a new catering company and an "all cruise" travel agency.

Remember – the zanier you think your idea is, the closer you are getting to a point of genius. Let your mind run wild. Have a brainstorming lunch with another business owner. You will be surprised at the willingness to explore ideas that can create differentiation and exposure to a larger client influence.

The Halo Effect

One of the more coveted benefits some alliances yield is creation of "the halo effect." It happens when one member of an alliance has created such an emotional attraction that it transfers equally to other partners. The result is an almost instant preference by association. On a national scale, you can catch a glimpse of this with Ben & Jerry's and Paul Newman, two highly visible corporate champions of causes.

The halo effect can be even more effective when the alliance is on a local basis. There are numbers of groups that are deeply dedicated to specific causes such as ethnic traditions, religious outreach or the gay/lesbian culture. Your community may have a tremendously active organization focused on minority- or female-owned businesses or a closely connected civic group that raises funds for environmental causes or disease research.

The halo effect only works if your heart is genuinely involved. If you are part of one of these groups, you know it right now. To be involved otherwise, solely for business purposes, will do more damage than good – and it will be irritating to everyone. If you find yourself questioning a prospective group's cohesive strength or influence, it probably isn't a legitimate candidate for conveying the "halo effect."

Halo-effect organizations are easily identifiable. Members regularly communicate. (They may have a monthly publication that you can write articles for.) They routinely get together for the "cause" and they actively know each other. If a group under consideration doesn't match up to those criteria, give it up. This does not mean you can't identify individuals within this group as people you can begin to connect with as future potential customers. It simply means that you may never be placed on that organization's proverbial pedestal as its preferred provider.

Once your targeted audience sees your strong identification to the group and you strategically accentuate your business specialty in this cohesive environment (Just knowing who

> *Branding requires leading your audience to a strong identification.*

you are isn't enough. They still need to know your business distinction), some customers will seek you out, some will continue to sit back and watch (but with growing interest) and some will talk to others about you. Most important, most – if not all – will eventually welcome your approach.

Branding requires leading your audience to a strong identification. To do that requires a local strategy of connection consistency, likability and differentiation. If you're going to achieve high-level success, you must create a belief that you're special, different and unique, relative to the competition.

Chapter Nine

Summary Reflections

If your customers rarely see or hear from you, market preference will not be established.

Business alliances can provide opportunities to connect more frequently, not only to your clients but also to new potential clients.

The more that customers interact, the greater chance they will establish a preference for you.

Don't focus on selling. Focus on your strategy that gets the customer to want to buy.

Repeat business requires more than just producing a satisfied customer at the time of the sale.

Great marketers embrace creativity – not market duplication.

What worked yesterday, won't work tomorrow. If it worked yesterday, it's probably not working today.

Be courageous! Embrace an idea that is exceptionally different than the competition and try it. If it's a flop, embrace another idea and try again. And if need be ... keep trying!

Branding always begins with an experience that creates a perception that you are incomparable, relative to the competition.

Separate yourself from the normal blandness of your competitors. Lead your audience to a strong identification with your differentiation.'

Brilliant Strategies Notebook

My thoughts on how to apply this chapter's lessons to my business...

"Creating market dominance is NOT all about service. Service keeps customers. Great service is critical. But, if you capture a new customer through service, it is because they are fleeing from a bad experience and you happen to be in their path of flight.

Creating market dominance requires more than just providing great service. It requires creative thinking."

Robert F. Krumroy

Chapter Ten

Common Oversights that Kill Retail Sales

How can you help people buy your products? What can you do externally that makes a difference in getting people to buy? Paco Underhill, the widely known retail anthropologist, lecturer and author of *Why We Buy – The Science of Shopping*, has extensively researched this topic and many of the following conclusions are based on his work, coupled with our work and observations. Though this section is not exhaustive, it is hoped that the applications and guidance will help make your small retail business a more desirable destination for shoppers and consequently also make a significant difference to your bottom line.

The successful small retail business opening today is not based on attracting customers by filling some consumer need. It's based on the belief that it must steal customers from the competition in order to survive. And once you lose a customer, chances are good that he or she is gone for good. So whether you are reading this book as a new business owner or an established business owner trying to get better, you better have an edge. You better have something more than just the ability to advertise a brand name product you happen to sell.

Your competition is trying to steal your customer.

And you better stay alert to reinventing your edge on a constant basis, lest the competition forges ahead of you at your expense.

As Paco Underhill has documented (and which should already be apparent to any retailer), the amount of time a shopper stays in a store is perhaps the single most important factor in determining how much she or he will buy. It has also been observed that "the more shopper-employee contacts that take place, the greater the average sale." What easy facts to consider; not ones we believe would solicit much different conclusions regardless of how long you would ponder them. However, it rarely appears that these strategic considerations are given much thought, and certainly not much thought that appears to result in any serious application. It almost appears in many stores that the obvious is the hardest to see. Yet the obvious, which is so frequently overlooked by most business owners, may prove to be your greatest strategy toward securing higher profits. But only if you act on the knowledge.

Keeping customers in your store requires one or more of the following elements: making an immediate and meaningful contact (more than "Can I help you") and keeping shoppers and companions entertained, intrigued or at the very least comfortable. Paco Underhill says "the amount of time a shopper spends in a store depends on how comfortable and enjoyable the experience is." It should go without saying that shoppers won't stay long if their companions are uncomfortable. As simple as these elements appear, however, they are more often than not overlooked.

The Initial "Can I Help You?" Customer Approach

In my opinion, there is no retail greeting that's more

meaningless and irritating than "Can I help you?" Whenever you begin a question with "Can ..." it naturally solicits a "yes" or "no" response. The response is virtually always going to be, "No, I'm just looking." If one could compare the level of stupidity of this comatose communication between the employee and the customer during this all-too-typical retailing encounter, I believe it would be a toss-up as to who would win. When will the retail owner understand that most customers are naturally defensive about "being sold," or maybe they are just naturally timid about interacting with someone they have never met. "No, I'm just looking" is always going to be the natural response to the thoughtless question, "Can I help you?"

No one is having any fun asking the same question, hearing the same predictable responses in the same way, with both parties irritated over exerting wasted energy in a meaningless interaction. There must be a better way.

In order for two people to be helpful to each other during an interaction, it is imperative that communication be considered *meaningful* and that both parties feel comfortable within the exchange. When one or both parties stop communicating, the ability to assist is halted. This is particularly frustrating during an initial selling encounter when one understands that a meaningful customer interaction results in more purchases and happier customers.

> *A meaningful initial customer interaction results in more purchases and happier customers.*

The solution to this uncomfortable dilemma is to learn to ask an "either-or" question that gives the customer a choice of two or three responses. Here's an example. "Hi. Welcome to the Silk Warehouse. Are you looking for blouses, skirts or dresses today?" If you have a dominant product or two, it won't be hard to settle on your choices. But even if your choices aren't what the customer is looking for, you will never hear the response, "No, I'm just looking."

> *Learn to ask an "either-or" question in your initial approach with the shopper.*

They will either pick one of your choices or they will say, "No, none of those." With that response, you now can ask, "What are you looking for?" (Never say, *"What can I help you with?"*) Be patient. Most will give you an answer.

The psychology behind the success of this question is that you have opened lines of communication by just allowing them to eliminate possible choices. Since they have already given you some information, they feel safer telling you what they are looking for. Emotionally, it feels much less threatening than responding to "Can I help you?"

Whether you have a hardware store, furniture store, computer store or clothing store, think about how you could train your salespeople to ask an "either-or" question at the initial interaction. You will see an immediate sales increase. You will also see more returning customers who appreciate the higher level of communication they receive.

The Waiting Game

Paco Underhill's research found that the single most important factor in customer satisfaction is the amount of time they are forced to cool their heels. "Few retailers realize that when shoppers are made to wait too long in line (or anywhere else), their impression of overall service plunges."

The following statement is hardly a revelation for most of us, but it appears to be a profound new piece of information for many storeowners: The longer a customer has to wait while checking out, the greater the chance they will not come back. It is true. Regardless of product quality or uniqueness of merchandise, there is a direct correlation between the amount of time shoppers have to wait in the checkout line and their final opinion about the quality of the place of business. And this conclusion is what determines whether they will return or find a different provider.

> *The longer a customer has to wait, the greater the chance they will not come back.*

My recent experience at a well-known national video rental store is a classic example of this. There were five employees in the store. Two were behind the counter, which housed four cash registers, but only one of them was checking out the long line of nine customers. After nine long minutes, the checkout procedure had turned potential happy customers into a disgruntled mob. If there was any satisfaction or happiness over finding the video they had shopped for, it had evaporated in the waiting line of dispirited shoppers. The man in front of me finally plunked down the three videos he was holding and stomped out of the store without a word. Not only was the sale lost, but who knows how many others he influenced by telling his story of incompetent service? I'm sure all of us in that line planned to share our negative experience with others.

There is no excuse for this happening in today's marketplace, yet it occurs far too often and the customer impact to your business is far from inconsequential. The customers are leaving and not coming back. There is nothing about waiting that makes a customer feel special or conveys a message that you want them to return. "When service is poor, shoppers will find another store," says Paco Underhill. "Bad service undoes good merchandise, prices and location almost every time."

How long is too long for waiting? It is a lot shorter than you think. According to Underhill's research, "When people wait up to about a minute and a half, their sense of how much time has elapsed is fairly accurate. Anything over ninety or so seconds, however, and their sense of time distorts – if you ask how long they've been waiting, their honest answer can often be a very exaggerated one. Taking care of a customer in two minutes is a success; doing it in three minutes is a failure."

> *The impression of your business is only as fresh as the customer's last encounter.*

There's never an excuse for giving customers a bad day. They don't care if some of your employees didn't show up. Their impression of your business is only as fresh as their last encounter, and a bad day can wipe out ten previous good encounters. Consistently great service comes with the territory of being a successful business owner. You have to live up to the expectation daily, or your customers will put you out of business. They will almost consider it their duty to society.

Fitting Room Waiting Areas

Addressed properly, this issue may be one of your best leverage points. Suggestion: Provide adequate seating outside the fitting rooms. Your fear of losing product space is insignificant compared to the sales you lose because customers' shopping companions are uncomfortable. If the shopping companions are comfortable, they will help sell more merchandise as it is "modeled," more than any amount of products you would have sold by increasing floor display space. Plus, if the waiting party is noticeably comfortable to the shopper, how much more comfortable will the shopping party be in extending their "product" consideration time?

I don't even want to think about how many times I've been forced to either lean against the wall or sit on the floor while waiting for my significant other to emerge from the fitting room. The fact is that most shoppers will end their shopping spree prematurely if their companions are not comfortable. In other words, not only do you want to give attention to the shopper but also to their companions.

> *Provide adequate seating for shopping companions.*

Add a few chairs! How simple a thought process this is, but so often overlooked. If your store attracts couples shopping together (husband and wife, girlfriend and boyfriend, woman and woman friend), provide adequate seating with comfortable surroundings. Even consider installing a television with video clips to entertain the waiters; that's not an expensive option.

Remember, we do know that the longer the person is detained in the store, the higher the reflection you will notice in sales. This is not a genius observation. It is common sense. So why is it so hard for storeowners to pay any attention to this simple little detail? Give us a place to sit, add a little entertainment (or something to look at) and we'll help you sell more merchandise than you ever would by jamming in more displays. Guaranteed!

> *The longer the shopper remains in your store, the greater the sales.*

Fitting Room Ambiance

Now, what about the fitting rooms themselves? The more comfortable people feel in the fitting room, the more time they are apt to take and the more clothes they will try on. And more time equals more sales. So why are fitting rooms so horribly maintained? Even in the best of stores, more times than not I've had to watch where I put my feet for fear of stepping on pins dropped by the last twenty people who unwrapped articles of clothing. God knows what lurks between the fibers of the carpet and under the clothes left on the floor, certainly not an environment that entices one to stay, linger, relax and enjoy the experience of trying on more merchandise.

> *Enticing fitting rooms encourage a shopping party to extend its time.*

Rarely do I find a fitting room that appears to have been vacuumed in the last two weeks. Why? Vacuums are not expensive. They could easily be made available for employees to use every hour if needed. What ever happened to common sense? Is it any mystery that clean, enticing fitting rooms might encourage a shopping party to extend its time, considerations and purchases?

To further the exasperation, some dressing rooms are so small you virtually cannot retrieve a dropped item. It's not an environment that encourages hunting for more merchandise to try on. Other fitting rooms are so non-private, adorned with little curtains that don't fit on both sides, that many customers are going to leave, simply because they don't share the same nonchalant attitude of "who cares if someone sees me" that you do.

In addition to the spatial and privacy issues, if by chance you do get the article of clothing on, how are you supposed to evaluate the look or the fit based on a mirror that's less than a foot away? If you want me to buy, give me an environment that welcomes me to stay and a mirror that allows me to see what I have placed on my body. And put some mirrors inside the fitting rooms. If I think I look bad, and I have to come out in the open to verify it, I'm not going to try many clothes on. Plus, I'll find another store to go to next time.

Additionally, add some mirrors all over the store. I have often left stores empty-handed because I either couldn't find a mirror, the mirror was too small (on a narrow post with clothing racks pressing against it) or someone else was using the *only* mirror. You'd think these were rationed artifacts and I should be tolerant of having to wait my turn to use them. Wake up, America's storeowners! Create an environment that seduces me. Give me some mirrors that are easy to access and a waiting room with a chair for my companion that welcomes them to stay and participate in my conquest. You just might increase your sales!

Shopping for retail is a seduction sport.

Shopping for retail is not like stopping to fill your car up with gasoline (a job one hopes can be done quickly). It is a seduction sport. Storeowners, do yourself a favor by enhancing your fitting rooms and waiting areas, even if you have to reduce your merchandise area. Paco Underhill's research proves that the extra sales would more than make up for the extra space that would demand. He states: "The dressing room may be more important than the floor of the store. It's a truism that improving the quality of dressing rooms increases sales. It never fails. A dressing room isn't just a convenience – it's a selling tool, like a display or a window or advertising. It sells more effectively than all of those combined, if it's properly used."

Finding and Accessing Fitting Rooms

A shopper's opinion of your store is only as good as his or her last experience. For many of us, it is only as good as our first experience, because that's all the chance you are going to get. One of the elements that will kill a potential sale quickly is not being able to find the fitting room. With the ability to design and purchase inexpensive attractive signs, there is no excuse for this, yet it is still a challenge for many. However, many times, not only can I not find the fitting rooms, but when I do find them, I can't find anyone with a key to let me access them. For a man, as well as many women, this is the final straw. I am not coming back.

The last time I checked, there is nothing in a dressing room that needs to be protected from being stolen. But the rebuttal is, "We are protecting our clothes from being shoplifted." Maybe so, but you are also losing sales because of customers leaving who are irritated by needing to find a clerk who can open the fitting room. How much have these lost sales and customers cost you? I can personally attest it has cost you a lot.

> *Unlock the fitting rooms. You will create happier customers and increased sales.*

Clothes are equipped with so many plastic alarms that would go off if you tried to steal them, I don't even understand why any old argument is still used. Unlock the fitting rooms and put some big signs up that tell me where the fitting rooms are located. You will see more appreciative customers and increased merchandise sales – more than the loss you will encounter through shoplifting.

Spatial Design

An entire book could be written about spatial design. It has a major effect on the perception of quality that we create in our minds during first encounters with a business, particularly a retail store. Sadly, it appears to be a topic that many business owners have spent little time studying. But the impact is critical, whether you're in the business of retail clothing, grocery, auto parts or any other tangible product business.

Paco Underhill has found that the front right of any store is its "prime real estate" because American shoppers automatically move to the right. For that reason, it's logical that your most important goods, "the make-or-break merchandise that needs one hundred percent shopper exposure," should go there. Some natural attention-grabbing merchandise should also be located at the back of the store. "Everyone knows why supermarket dairy cases are usually against the back wall," says Underhill. "It's because almost every shopper needs milk, and so they'll pass through (and shop) the entire store on the way to and from the rear." That's the same reason drugstores put their pharmacies at the back.

Endcaps on rows are often overlooked, yet they're some of the most effective places to display goods. "An endcap can boost an item's sales simply because as we stroll through a store's aisles, we approach them head-on, seeing them plainly and fully," explains Underhill. The degree of creating customer appeal with an endcap also increases the number of customers who travel down the entire aisle.

And finally, one of my pet peeves (and apparently one that disturbs Underhill just as much) is the width of space between aisle rows. We all have an aversion to winding our way down aisles that are crowded, even in a grocery store. But

> *Put customer comfort ahead of product display and floor space utilization.*

put a number of people in a clothing store, where we have to turn sideways in order to pass someone else, and you are going to stop the shopping experience prematurely. We are going to leave the store. No one is going to "linger" in a crowded aisle. Get bumped a couple of times and see what happens. If I feel uncomfortable, I leave without buying what I came in for, much less what I might have purchased by staying longer.

So why do stores squeeze their aisles with merchandise or uncomfortably narrow the passage space between rows? There are several theories. One is that they're ignorantly more concerned with store function than customer comfort, a throwback to the days of male-dominated hardware stores. Another is that they fear wasting space. Maybe nobody has told them that people are more concerned with the experience than the product. Regardless of the reason, a lot can be learned by looking at your spatial design. If fifteen percent less product display space results in one hundred percent more customer comfort, you will be able to substantially increase sales.

Sidewalk Display Windows

Can this really be a major attractor or distractor? Yes. Display windows communicate far more than a sampling of products your store carries. They send a resounding message that is far louder and has a far deeper impact than most business owners ever realize. The implied message that every customer knows, but seems to be so unknown to the average business owner is this: When I see the same display in your window over and over, I know that there is nothing interesting happening in your store. There is no reason to go in to investigate. I am certainly not going in to just "look."

Yes, that is the message. The frequency by which you change your display windows is equal to the degree of interest you will generate for me to want to return and "look again." You can't afford to transmit an unconscious message that your store is stagnant and has little happening by maintaining the same display. It is not the product display that sends the message or

> *The frequency by which you change your display windows is equal to the degree of interest you will generate.*

creates an irresistible appeal for the customer. It is the visible communication that something must be changing; there must be new merchandise inside; people must be buying out the old stuff; this must be a dynamic store; I better get in to look or I could miss out. Change your display windows at least monthly. Semi-weekly is better. Weekly is better than better. Daily? Do some stores really change their display windows daily? Ask the Thousand O' Prints store in Greensboro, NC. Every morning their display window has different prints displayed. You can't help but look to see what is new. Is it any wonder that they are consistently profitable and one of the oldest surviving businesses in downtown Greensboro.

Recommended Reading:
If you are a retail storeowner, make sure you read the following book, *Why We Buy – The Science of Shopping,* by Paco Underhill. Not only is it a national bestseller, but it is a book that is full of insightful tips that can result in greater sales, greater customer preference and greater market dominance.

Chapter Ten

Summary Reflections

The newly established successful business didn't become successful by looking for new customers. They became successful by stealing someone else's customer.

You better stay alert, constantly reviewing and reinventing your market differentiation, which gave you your initial competitive edge.

If you're a retail storeowner, your greatest boost in sales will occur if you figure out how to keep your customers in your store longer.

Stop asking, "Can I help you?' Learn to encounter the customer with an "either – or" question to create more meaningful interaction and greater sales.

Waiting in a checkout line will ruin your reputation faster than any other single element.

The more companion-comfortable your fitting room waiting areas are, the more merchandise you will sell. Add some chairs for companion comfort and watch your sales soar.

Shopping is a seduction sport. Don't repel the contestants by your lack of attention to your fitting room ambiance. A great fitting room experience can out-class your competition, or vice-a-versa.

Unlock the fitting rooms! Put up highly visible signs telling me where they are located.

The frequency that you change your outside display window is in direct proportion to the amount of customer traffic you receive - a simple fact, too often ignored.

Brilliant Strategies Notebook

My thoughts on how to apply this chapter's lessons to my business...

"Understanding marketing is not sufficient. Your future success will be dependent on *implementing* a well thought out marketing strategy or you will need to prepare for an alternative career.

In today's competitive marketplace, these are the only two choices."

Robert F. Krumroy

Let's Get Started

You are about to embark on the most exciting business challenge that you will ever confront – the new marketing revolution that is gripping America. This consumer change will be the stuff from which generational stories are made. It will be like sitting on your great-great-great-grandfather's lap and hearing about the first airplane he ever saw fly overhead. It will be like seeing the first broadcast TV show or the first one shown in color.

However, this change is not about a new revolutionary product being developed and introduced to the public. This change is not just about consumers wanting more information, wanting to be treated more professionally or wanting to know more about the reasoning behind your recommendations. This change is about the consumer being more skeptical, being tired of all the advertising clutter and yet having more alternatives than ever before for purchasing anything and everything they may want. It is about the consumer being in control of directing the buying and the selling process. Your old focus on trying to sell to the customer will need to be refocused on getting the customer to want to buy from you.

This challenge requires a response to meeting customers' demands for both greater intimacy and then providing what they want, when they want it, where they want it and how they want it. You have an opportunity not only to survive this change but to prosper from it. But truthfully, most will fail. Survival is dependent upon your ability to adopt and adapt. You learn by doing, not by cautiously plotting and planning. You learn by making decisions and implementing changes. Resiliency is key. Quick decisions, coupled with resiliency when errors are made, are far superior to good decisions implemented six months too late. Speed is critical. Delaying is fatal.

> *Building greater customer intimacy must become a priority.*

Your effectiveness in creating market dominance by demonstrating that your product and service are superior to the competition, has diminished or perhaps totally vanished. Acquiring market dominance and preference is no longer a by-product of being good at what you do. You acquire it by consciously strategizing how to build your appeal, differentiate your image and increase your attraction *(Identity Branding)*.

> *Achieving market dominance is not about being good at what you do. It's far more.*

Today, visibility in your marketplace is intentionally produced. It doesn't just happen. A purchase today is less about product than ever before. It's likely that the product you sell is no more singularly defined than McDonald's® defining hamburgers as its business. Someone once said that if McDonald's had defined itself as hamburgers, the chain would have failed; in a hamburger competition, it would have come out last.

McDonald's attraction is built from the same foundation that your future needs to be built from: the formulation of a distinct personality, created and maintained through a differentiated experience. Your success will only be sustained by your ability to continually astonish the customer, over and over and over again – three to four times a year. It will require that you constantly razzle and dazzle your audience, improving on your marketing strategy, and constantly creating brilliant ways to connect with your customers. Great marketing is never based on one idea or one event. It is based on a multiplicity of things that consistently astonish the customer and create attraction.

> *Today's customer wants to be continually astonished.*

Success is no longer about setting a strategy to get closer to the customer. It is about getting the customer closer to you. The message is loud and clear: to survive and thrive, you can no longer afford to look like another "Me-Too" company. If you're found guilty of that, the consumer won't allow you to survive. They will quickly see your "sameness" and apply the appropriate response – avoidance.

The approaches in this book are far from exhaustive in illustrating ways to become unique, distinct and dominant within your local market. However, they point the way to the sort of activities and strategies that are required if you are to succeed in this new consumer environment. The challenge for your future success does not lie in yesterday's traditional methods of conducting business or in believing that your product, even if you can prove that it is "the best," will eventually get noticed and rise to the top. Rather, future success lies in the hands of those

> *The traditional marketing attitude of yesterday won't even get you noticed today.*

businesses that focus on attraction marketing, implementing meaningful strategies and ultimately answering the consumer's question, "Why You?"

> *The customer has to answer the question, "Why you?" ... and why not the competition.*

So, how do you get started? The first step as a business owner is to not delegate creating a branding strategy to someone else. You must be personally and fully involved. Listen to your intuition. Mold the strategy to who you are and make sure you stay on course.

Second, strategize a distinction deliverable, a differentiator, relative to the competition! A distinction deliverable is an attribute that is characteristically distinct, unique and noticeably attributable to you. You can't own a distinction that someone else already owns. Be creative. Be unconventional. Be fun. Be likable. People like to be surprised and delighted. They crave to be part of an experience that is unique.

> *Be creative. Be unconventional. Be fun.*

Be first among your competitors in claiming a differentiation, one that can create a distinct appeal to the public. And don't be modest. Claim it and then shout it from the rooftops! Differentiators must be public. They must be visible. However, most differentiators have nothing to do with your product. The flood of "Me-Too" products and services in society is still rising with no end in sight. Even if you could create a product advantage, it would be short-lived, maybe six weeks before someone else has it and has improved on it.

Granted, "first" always has the advantage of becoming the most popular and the highest recognizable brand within its category. First is always better than better, but "first" for the local business may have more to do with how you deliver yourself to the customer, versus a characteristic about your product or service. However, if you do have a chance of becoming first with a product, for heaven's sake don't delay. Remember Coke? Pepsi only wishes they could have been first.

Create consistent familiarity.

Third, identify your name-specific audience and create a strategy to keep in consistent communication. You can't win a "courting match" or a "likability contest" if you don't create consistent familiarity. Your audience wants to be surprised and delighted and feel that you really care – and not just when you're providing a service or selling a product to them. They will develop an emotional bond with those who display affection and attention to them most often, and in ways that are uniquely different and surprising.

Attraction marketing is critical if you are going to survive.

Above all, don't get sidetracked. Don't allow marketing to be a secondary focus. Your attention to *attraction marketing* will determine if your company is known as a survivor because of your brilliant strategy or as another fatality because of your fatal blunders. *Attraction marketing* is critical to your future success. If you strategize and implement correctly, your business will flourish. Yes, even in an overcrowded marketplace.

Chapter Eleven

Summary Reflections

The consumer is causing the biggest marketing change ever witnessed in modern history.

Your focus must change from trying to sell to trying to get the customer to want to buy.

You will need to focus not on producing a satisfied customer, that won't be enough, but rather on ways to astonish them three to four times per year.

Survival will require strategizing to increase your appeal; to differentiate yourself from the competition and to create a distinct business personality.

Be creative. Be unconventional. Be fun. Be likable.

Today's customer is far less concerned about why your product or service. They are more concerned with "why you?" Differentiation has far more to do with how you deliver your perceived package of value to the customer.

If success is to be your destiny, somewhere along the road you will have out-strategized the competition and answered the customer's question, "WHY YOU?"

Brilliant Strategies Notebook

My thoughts on how to apply this chapter's lessons to my business...

_____

_____

_____

_____

_____

_____

_____

_____

_____

_____

_____

_____

_____

_____

_____

_____

_____

_____

_____

_____

_____

_____

_____

_____

References and
Acknowledgements

Krumroy, Robert E. (*Identity Branding: Distinct or Extinct*) (Greensboro, NC: I-B Publishing, 1999)

Schmitt, Bernd and Simonson, Alex (*Marketing Aesthetics*) (New York, NY: The Free Press, 1997)

Treacy, Michael and Wiersema, Fred (*The Discipline of Market Leaders*) (Reading, MA: Addison-Wesley Publishing Company, 1995)

Trout, Jack with Steve Rivkin (*Differentiate or Die*) (New York, NY: John Wiley & Sons, Inc., 2000)

Underhill, Paco (*Why We Buy*) (New York, NY: Touchstone Book, Simon & Schuster, 2000)

Upshaw, Lynn (*Building Brand Identity*) (New York, NY: John Wiley & Sons, Inc., 1995)

Zyman, Sergio (*The End of Marketing as We Know It*) (New York, NY: Harper Collins, 2000)

About the Author

Robert Krumroy, known as "The Branding Coach," is president and CEO of Identity Branding Inc. He is also founder and creator of the e-mail marketing tools www.emailconcept.com and www.my-ecustomer.com. Identity Branding is devoted to helping business owners and professionals create a visibly distinct and unique local market presence, a perception of superior value – eventually creating an almost unfair competitive advantage for themselves. Once accomplished, these businesses can thrive in a market flooded with competition and successfully compete for customers who are harder to attract than at any time in history.

With a degree in sociology, Krumroy began his career in 1973 as a financial service professional, specializing in working with small business owners. He qualified sixteen times as a National Management Award winner and built his financial service firm into one of the one-hundred largest in the country. He is the author of two books, numerous columns and magazine articles. He has served on national teaching faculties and is a highly sought after speaker, giving more than one hundred clinics and speeches each year to clients that include some of the largest companies in America. Widely considered one of the best marketing minds in the country,

Krumroy offers a wide range of resources for business owners, educational organizations and professionals.

For more information:

www.identitybranding.com

You can also call, e-mail, write or fax:

Identity Branding Inc.
2007 Yanceyville Rd., Suite 270
Greensboro, NC 27405

Toll free: 1.800.851.8169
Fax: 1.336.303.7318
E-mail: Bob@identitybranding.com

To Order Books

Please mail or fax this form to the address below, or use the electronic order form found at www.identitybranding.com.

_____ copies at $18.95 each = _____
($18.95 US; $24.95 CAN)

Plus $3.00 shipping/handling = _____
($3.00 US; $5.00 CAN)

Total Enclosed = _____

Please send book(s) to:

Name_____

Address _____

City _____ State _____ Zip _____

Method of payment:

❏ VISA   ❏ MasterCard

Credit Card number:_____

Expiration Date_____

Phone Number (   ) _____

Card Holder's Signature _____

Order on our Web site or by sending credit card, check or money order to:

Identity Branding
2007 Yanceyville Street, Suite 270
Greensboro, NC 27405

Fax: 336-303-7318
E-mail: info@identitybranding.com
www.identitybranding.com